PRAISE FOR UNSEALED

by Mark Greene
with Shelby Rawson

My friend, BUD/S Classmate, and SEAL Teammate Mark Greene has captured the lessons from his earliest days, the SEAL Teams, combat, and his transition into the private sector in his new book *UNSEALED*—an open, honest, unflinching account of a life in the trenches, one that will inspire you to build upon your own foundation and achieve your full potential. Make Mark's journey part of yours—then get to work crushing all you do! Read *UNSEALED* today!

—**Jack Carr**
Navy SEAL Sniper and #1 New York Times
bestselling author of *Only the Dead*

For anyone seeking the skills to overcome adversity, Mark Greene, a former Navy SEAL and college football player, lays out the roadmap. This was a must-read for me as it is for you.

—**Jeff Pegues**
CBS News Chief National Affairs and Justice Correspondent, author, and host of *America Changed Forever* on SiriusXM Potus Channel

Courage isn't the absence of fear, rather, it's the ability to step into our fear. Few understand the courage it takes to pivot in life, make a hard turn, transition from certainty into uncertainty. Mark's narrative in

UNSEALED about his own transition from the military is remarkably ubiquitous, not because we all have to transition, but because we all have to face fear. Mark is a gem, and this book is too!

—**Rich Diviney**
Bestselling author of *The Attributes*
Retired Navy SEAL Commander

What sets this book apart is the author's authenticity and vulnerability. Mark does not shy away from sharing the difficult moments of his transition journey, including the moments of doubt, fear, and sadness. He also shares the moments of hope, love, and triumph that made his transition journey possible.

I have known Mark Greene for over twenty years, and I can honestly say that he is one of the strongest, most resilient individuals I have ever met. His journey through transition is not unique, but it is a powerful testament to the strength of the human spirit and the importance of the support of loved ones and community.

His experiences with military transition, a long career, athletics at the collegiate level, divorce, visible and invisible wounds associated with prolonged service and multiple combat tours, the loss of loved ones, and the support he received that helped him successfully transition are incredibly moving and relatable. His story is a reminder that we all face transitions in our lives and that it is possible to emerge stronger and more resilient on the other side.

—**Mark Owen**
Bestselling author of *No Easy Day*
Executive Producer of the hit TV show *SEAL Team* on *CBS*

One of my biggest takeaways from Mark's talk is how "you are where you are supposed to be." Sometimes I would feel like what I am doing can be meaningless and feeling lost as a college student, but reflecting on my past and my achievements, I can definitely say that many of my achievements are not overnight and are made up of thousands of right decisions. I think it is an important mindset to have that everything you do is significant and having the right mindset will get you to where you want to go.

—**USC Student**

Mark taught me that when you reframe the lessons from your own life as surmountable challenges, rather than being paralyzed by the fear of self-doubt, you can begin to turn unbreakable barriers into manageable obstacles.

—**USC Student**

Though Mark's presence and personal story alone gave me a deeper insight into how I could deal with my own personal issues, what struck me most is how he dealt with hardship throughout his life and the value he places on the community surrounding him at any given moment. He made it clear that in order to grow, you must look to surround yourself with not only like-minded people, but also with driven, lively, and inquisitive people who are willing to reflect and expand on ideas rather than echo them.

—**USC Student**

UNSEALED

A Navy SEAL's Guide to Mastering Life's Transitions

MARK GREENE

WITH SHELBY RAWSON

For permissions requests, speaking inquiries, and bulk order purchase options, email: markgreeneauthor@gmail.com.

Greene UNSEALED LLC
160 2nd Avenue South
Nashville, TN 37201
themarkgreene.com

ISBN: 979-8-9890682-8-9

Designed by Transcendent Publishing | TranscendentPublishing.com
Edited by Lori Lynn Enterprises
Cover photo by Emily Paszczykowski

**This book is lovingly dedicated to my father,
James Shirley Greene, Jr.**

My father often said …

"Son, make sure you do things a little bit better every day."

Those words have shaped and influenced everything I do in life.

Although he will never have the chance to see the final product of his love, guidance, mentorship, consistency, kindness, loyalty, and generosity, I am honored and eternally grateful to have had such a powerful man in my life.

He shaped almost every aspect of the man I am today, and "thank you" will never be enough to encompass everything he provided for me, my brother, sister, and mother.

His legacy lives on in the pages of this book.

"There is no illusion greater than fear."

—Lao Tzu

CONTENTS

FOREWORD

Imagine what it takes when we are at our worst, to say with conviction, "I am right where I need to be." By affirming that we are where we need to be, we put some distance from the sting of what is happening, and think, Well, this sucks ... But if I am where I need to be, how can I learn from it?

This is a necessary component for anyone who wants to live fully. But when we are really in the thick of things, the ability to step back and reflect requires an overwhelming amount of mental fortitude.

Mark's story teaches us how to face this challenge.

His willingness to remove the ego and the subjective self from the narrative of pain and failure puts his circumstances into a perspective where learning and growth can happen. As a neuroscientist, the term I would use for this is "metacognition," which refers to how we think about our thinking.

While my life's focus is on how people regulate emotion, my passion is to explore the good life: how we can best pursue big things, build deep relationships, and savor both good and bad experiences.

In addition to learning from other scientists and mentors, I've seen firsthand how pressure and life transition uncover our most durable selves and painfully strip away the facade of purposeless narrative.

Through this journey, I have made a few conclusions which I call "The Hard Three."

1. There's nothing outside of ourselves that can fix something inside, and vice versa, our inner selves, properly developed, need little from the outside world in order to flourish.

2. Optimism is how we think about using our resources, not how hopeful we are that things will turn out for the better, and

3. Gratitude is the most important virtue to cultivate for high performance, especially during challenging times.

I call these the Hard Three because they are not the fluffy version of gratitude, purpose, and optimism that are embroidered on your pillows and doilies. These three precepts will torment and taunt us.

- We know they are true, yet why do we still wait until things are good to practice gratitude?

- Why do we blindly hope things will get better without changing something we can do?

- Why do we get on the hedonic treadmill hoping for meaning and validation from our next purchase, meal, drink, or social media post?

These are tremendous challenges, but to the degree they can be tamed, they are game-changing for control of our life and its narrative. It requires a self-distancing from the events that happen to us which remove our ego, focus on what matters, bind us with others, and give ourselves compassion and permission to be where we want to be. I am by far no master of the Hard Three, so I am drawn to people and experiences that can teach me a new angle or a new perspective on them.

Mark is one of these people.

Mark's story is about so much more than life as a Navy SEAL. In fact, I might argue that being a SEAL is only the surface of what makes Mark so interesting.

Mark's stories teach us about life in really profound ways. His decision to enlist in the Navy while working at Blockbuster Video is a showcase of optimism.

His mental framework for getting through BUD/S by saying "I'm just playing at the beach with my friends" teaches us about how our internal story beats our external circumstances every time.

His time in the teams and his difficult transition afterward are all about gratitude. In fact, nearly every story Mark tells has a deep connection to gratitude—especially to his innate ability to connect with others.

I have so many Mark Greene stories, and I am delighted that you will have the chance to hear them too. May they also help anyone's transition to better purpose, optimism, and gratitude.

Glenn R. Fox, PhD
Assistant Professor of Clinical Entrepreneurship
Lloyd Greif Center for Entrepreneurial Studies
USC Marshall School of Business

1

FEAR OF THE UNKNOWN

"The brave man is not he who does not feel afraid, but he who conquers that fear."

—Nelson Mandela

Man, if I die down here, I'm gonna be so pissed. As I pressed against the invisible hand that held me beneath the surface of the ocean, all I could do was sit there and hope for rescue.

With the ship's propellors above me and the threat of sharks all around me, I looked up from the middle of the ocean with the full realization that I was on the verge of losing my life.

I had already survived one near-death experience, and now I was trying desperately to survive another.

Twenty years of high-stakes situations like this couldn't prepare me for the change I was about to face as I transitioned from being a Navy SEAL back to being a civilian, plummeting headlong from the familiar into the unknown.

To tell the truth, I was terrified.

The moment I finally admitted my terror took me by surprise. I was attending an event for a nonprofit that supports special operators and their families.

Given my background in special ops, I'm always on the lookout for bad things to happen. As a result, I've never been a huge fan of big cities. But here I was, in New York, feeling overwhelmed by all the things that make the Big Apple such an amazing place.

There's the constant noise that starts off as a chaotic cacophony of car horns, police sirens, screeching tires, and the sounds of the Metro. Who can escape the throng of what seems like all humanity stuffed inside a sardine can?

As I settle in, though, the chaos fades into an almost pleasant background noise that has proven to be a typical urban symphony.

One of my many layers of defense relaxes. But just as one threat is identified and dismissed, more emerge.

The onslaught of gasoline, street vendors, a foreign language I've never heard, live musicians, and the controlled ballet of people rushing to places unknown as fast as they can ... these sounds are once again categorized as normal, and I continue my walk toward the most important meeting I've ever had.

The next stage of anxiety and threat control comes in the form of meticulously scrutinizing the body language of all the potential threats who are mere inches from me.

My training and my preferred method of dealing with threats from the past nineteen years must be put in check because I can't start punching New Yorkers in the face for getting too close to me. I'm a visitor and I'm on their turf.

The final frontier is dodging all the cars and buses meandering through the streets. In highly populated urban areas, street signs and traffic signals are often taken as suggestions instead of rules.

At one point, I even had to grab my wife at the time by the shoulder. In the midst of her awe with the city, she came dangerously close to losing a battle with a 2,000-pound car.

Now that all of my threats have been identified and categorized as "non-threats," there was still something that kept me on high alert, as if I were in some kind of danger.

Normally, I didn't pay much attention to the constant but urgent "buzz" in my body. (If you've never experienced it, this sensation is kind of like drinking an energy drink that lights you up, but not so much as to stop you from being normal—just feels like a little shot of adrenaline.)

The buzz had been my constant companion and was almost always welcome because we had been together for so long. Now that it was no longer needed for combat situations, it should have quieted down. Yet, there it was, getting louder and more urgent the closer I got to the venue.

The moment I stepped into the dimly lit atrium of the restaurant, I felt completely out of place. I had arrived a little early, which meant that none of my teammates were there yet to offer the kind of comfort that only fellow special operators can provide.

As I'm standing there feeling exposed and vulnerable, a very kind gentleman strikes up a conversation with me. He's fascinated by my story since I'm the first Navy SEAL he's ever met. Little do I know, he is about to introduce me to the man who will become my "Sea Daddy" and serve as my mentor for the next several years.

The friendly stranger asks the question that I have yet to be asked in all my time in the SEAL Teams.

"How do you feel about retiring soon?"

Without even thinking, I blurt out, "I'm terrified!"

Terror didn't even scratch the surface of what was on its way. I was sitting front and center as a spectator of my very own upcoming train wreck.

All the challenges and environments that we elite warriors face suddenly paled in comparison to the harsh realities of transitioning from military service to the civilian world.

Over the course of my career, I had learned to adapt and succeed at the highest level under some of the worst possible conditions. Yet, the realization that I was plummeting at full speed toward a fate that I wasn't prepared for was its own unique form of terror.

I wasn't ready to leave the SEAL "locker room." Life without my tribe seemed unimaginable. I definitely wasn't ready to leave the purpose-driven life that I'd grown to need and love. And in no way did I feel prepared to embark on a new journey without a clear mission.

It is difficult to describe the palpable shock on people's faces when I was asked how I felt about my new life outside of the military.

I started my career as an enlisted SEAL and made the transition to become a Navy SEAL officer. I had completed my bachelor's degree, earned a master's degree, and was a combat veteran completing special operations missions and sniper missions under incredibly arduous and dangerous conditions.

With my accomplishments, I should have been prepared for what was to come—but I wasn't. I didn't even know what I was good at without the comforting blanket of my SEAL Team, my teammates, and my expertise.

There I was, feeling naked and afraid, engulfed in uncertainty, fumbling my way through a maze that I was not equipped to successfully navigate.

To say that I was unprepared is an understatement.

But before we dive into that story, let's go back to the beginning.

2

VISIONS OF GREATNESS

Walking up the stairs to my grandparents' old, green house in Youngstown, Ohio, I had to pass the gauntlet of the mulberry tree. There were always berries on the ground, and it smelled terrible.

As an 8-year-old kid, I used to curl my nose up and try to hold my breath, but somehow, the scent of those berries crept into my nose. I remember closing my eyes and puffing out my cheeks and I held my breath.

Once the smell dissolved, I'd walk up to the front porch and into the house. Through the front door, I could see all the way through the kitchen. Off to the right was the dining room chair that nobody else was allowed to sit in. It was my grandfather's workstation and the place where he would always watch TV.

Off to the left was the black-and-white TV. Sticking out of the top of that old thing was the antenna wrapped in tinfoil. Most of the channels flickered, but the channel that had the baseball game was crystal clear.

One day, I was surprised to see my grandpa sitting there watching TV. Out of the blue, he says, "Boy, get over here and sit down."

As an 8-year-old shy and quiet kid, if I wasn't at his house riding in circles on my bike for hours, I was either playing with my cousins or doing something other than sitting in a house watching baseball.

I didn't really want to sit down. What I wanted was to go see my grandma because whenever I would go over there, she'd say, "Boy, come get some of this cake!"

She always baked this wonderful yellow cake while she cooked up some collard greens or some other good ol' Southern fare. I used to love to come in and have my grandma tell me to sit down and eat.

This time, though, my grandpa spoke to me. I'm pretty sure this is the first conversation we ever had.

He says, "You know you have a good arm, and I want to teach you how to play baseball. We're going to go outside and we're gonna practice, and I'm gonna teach you how to pitch."

I think, *"Ooh! I love to play outside. I'd love to play baseball!"*

Then he says, "Before we go, I want you to watch a baseball game."

And I think, *"Ok, I'll sit and watch a game, but I don't know where I'll sit."*

Grandpa's wooden seat looks like a throne. All the other chairs are smaller, and they're pretty far away from his main chair, but he pulls up one of the smaller wooden chairs. It's the kind with a mesh back that makes you sit up straight.

"You're gonna come over here and sit with me, boy."

"Yessir." I climb into the chair and sit next to my grandpa. I don't want to make eye contact with him because I think he's mean. (Turns out, he wasn't mean at all, but I sure didn't know that back then!)

As the game is getting ready to start, he says, "This is going to be a great game. Now, boy, I don't know if you know this, but I used to pitch in the Negro Leagues."

Not knowing what that means, I just say, "Oh, ok."

The baseball game starts, and he's trying to explain the game to me, and he's excited in a way that I've never seen him excited before.

I'm taking in the moment of being with my grandpa who, up to now, I thought didn't like me. He's just having a fit over there, and I am utterly unimpressed.

The game ends up having almost no action. One pitcher pitches a no-hitter and the other pitcher pitches a one- or a two-hitter. It was torture.

Here I am thinking that I'm getting ready to go out and play this game of baseball and I sit through nine innings of one of the worst sporting events I'd ever seen.

In the meantime, all this food's cooking, the cake is waiting for me, my cousins are out playing ...

And my grandpa is really into watching this game. He even has his baseball mitt with him. He puts the glove on, and, like baseball players do, he balls up his pitching fist and keeps pounding the glove.

I'm thinking, "*There's no way I am ever gonna play baseball.*" I feel like it's almost a wasted experience because he's *so* excited, and I'm so bored.

By the end of the game, I say, "Grandpa, I don't ever want to play baseball." I hop up, go to the kitchen, eat some cake, and never look at baseball again.

He never showed it, but I think he was disappointed that I wasn't interested in the game that he fell in love with.

This old man, that I thought didn't even like me, was sharing his sacred love of the game with his grandson. Today I can see that he loved me enough to want to share those moments of throwing the baseball, like most dads and sons would do back then.

The combination of sights, sounds, and events from that day burned into my memory. To this day, I don't think I've ever seen my grandpa that excited.

I remember later on at his funeral, *years* later, they talked about how much of a baseball fan he was. When they said he played for the Negro Leagues, I was finally at an age where I understood what that meant, and I still kick myself because he was so excited to teach me to play baseball, and I was so turned off by how boring that stupid game was that I wanted nothing to do with it.

That poor man was ready to ignite in me a love of baseball, but he accidentally did the opposite by having me watch a boring game. What's interesting is that I would later sit and watch something else that would have the opposite effect, sparking a clear vision for my future.

Before that, though, my life plan was to go to the NFL and be the next great black quarterback. Starting out as the grandson of a professional baseball pitcher, I didn't know it, but I had athlete DNA. My grandpa knew it, though, and I'd put in the hours and worked really hard.

I ended up playing football in college, and he was proud of me because I had such a strong arm and I played quarterback, so he was happy that I used that super strong arm for something.

At the time, I was in college trying to earn a coveted football scholarship. I played quarterback at Miami University (Miami of Ohio) and Kent State University. When I was at Kent State, everything was going pretty well. I seemed to be progressing right on track to be the next Randall Cunningham or Colin Kaepernick. Just pick your black quarterback and I was going to be that guy in the NFL.

My plans to go pro came to a screeching halt the day I suffered a catastrophic shoulder injury. It took years to regain full mobility. In the blink of an eye, my football career ended along with all of my hopes and dreams of playing football at the highest level. I was devastated.

I had no backup plan. I started to lose my drive. I didn't know where to put my focus. I hadn't planned to get injured and get thrown completely out of the game. All of a sudden, I was stuck not knowing what to do next.

But then one day, a close friend of mine named Jeff says, "Hey, Mark. You're a great quarterback, you're a good dude, and I think we should try to do this thing called Navy SEALs."

I didn't even know what that meant back in 1991. There was no YouTube, no BUD/S online class to learn about Navy SEALS. There was a docuseries on the Discovery Channel, but I didn't see that until 2003, and I graduated BUD/S in 1997. It was just the blind leading the blind, two clueless guys encouraging each other to go be a SEAL.

I had never heard of BUD/S, which, in case you've never heard of it either, BUD/S (Basic Underwater Demolition/SEAL training) is the 26-week training course designed to develop regular sailors into one of America's most elite fighting forces and the premier maritime special operations forces in the world. These men are commonly known as Navy SEALs.

My buddy Jeff kept telling me, "These guys are the best of the best in the military and in the world. They do the hardest missions, they have the hardest training, and all you have to do to survive and be a SEAL is to not quit the training."

My mom's voice kept playing in my head. I could hear her saying, "Son, you're gonna do great things." I had thought my "great thing" was football, so when I didn't have that, I didn't know what my opportunities were to "be great."

I was in college, and it wasn't really what I wanted to do. College was being used as a means to an end. My hopes of a football career had ended, which meant my reason for being in college did, too.

So, when Jeff sat me down and told me, "Look, before we go any further, there's this really great video about the SEALs and what they do in the training." And when he turned on the video, I wasn't bored for a single second. *I was mesmerized.*

The training looked awful. The dedication and 70 to 80 percent attrition rate spoke to me (even though that seems contradictory!). I wanted to do something special, and the title of the video was, "Be Someone Special."

I kept thinking, "*Oh man, that sounds like a great idea.*"

Watching that video sparked the beginning of my obsession.

This was seven years before my own SEAL career ever started.

I didn't know it then, but what I've discovered since is that the people who want to take that route have to be completely obsessed with it. They have to give it 90 to 100 percent of their time, energy, and attention. It has to dominate their thoughts. It takes unwavering dedication.

As a 21-year-old college kid who moved from place to place as an Air Force brat, I had no idea what that level of dedication looked like. I just knew that the light had switched on for what I wanted to do and what I wanted to become.

Throughout my life, I had always been told that I had to live up to my potential ... I had this voice in my head saying, "Do not underachieve or disappoint people by not giving your best effort in everything you do ..." I would often look around at the world around me and ask myself, *What's going to help me do that?*

Once I watched that video, I set my sights on being a SEAL. But since my injury, I still had several years of college left, so I continued to go through school. I wasn't there to learn anything, though. I was there to play football. Since that was stripped away, I lost motivation, I lost focus, and I flunked out.

Now, not only was I an injured athlete but I was also a 23-year-old college dropout. My options for greatness were looking pretty bleak. My identity as a star athlete got stripped away. My identity as a college student failed miserably. Now I'm just a dude living in Cincinnati trying to figure out how to put his best efforts into something meaningful.

What my body and mind were aching for was something exciting, but what I was doing was pretty damn mediocre. I was working part-time jobs at bookstores and a little place called Blockbuster Video. (I looked great with that name tag.)

There I was at Blockbuster Video in my blue khakis and my light blue shirt with my name tag, while also working around the University of Cincinnati. It was fun to work there, but it was not a career. I still knew that I wanted to be a SEAL, but I had lost my drive.

I was starting to go down the road of, "Hey, this is okay. I'll get a job interview, and I'll work in corporate America somewhere. Then, at some point, I'll finish my degree." But as I said, I didn't really have a plan. I had nothing finite, nothing definitive. Nothing.

I was sinking into a depression because I was afraid to succeed. I had an almost overwhelming fear of success. Although that fear was always present, I was not willing to remain stuck where I was.

While I was working random part-time jobs, the outside world looked at me and said I wasn't achieving much at all. My life was ordinary and unremarkable in every way.

With a deep desire to blend in with the background, I was just floundering. I was going through the motions of what I thought I was "supposed to do."

What I didn't realize then is that Blockbuster Video would be the perfect catalyst to compel me to stop what I was doing, refocus, and take steps toward a new path.

People renting movies from Blockbuster will stand around and talk movies, and it was my job to make sense of some very obscure references, often made by a tipsy college student ... "Hey, do you know this one scene about this one guy and this one thing?"

Based on that alone, I could rattle off the name of the movie. It was kind of a joke because I was pretty good at taking the little bit of nothing that the customers told me and quickly finding what they needed.

Still, the work itself was nothing anybody could be a professional at, nothing that really tested my abilities. It was just another day at work for me when I was standing in Blockbuster, looking at the "Be Kind, Please Rewind" sign.

(If this were a screenplay instead of a book, you'd see a flashback of me riding my bike in circles, sitting with my grandpa watching a boring baseball game, destroying my shoulder, and watching that exhilarating Navy SEALS video ... the montage of memories would be interrupted by a ridiculous clown walking in to rent a movie.)

This guy is dressed like some kind of pimp with a top hat, a cane, and a loud, awful suit. If a suit could look at you and scream, "I'm hideous!" it was this one.

He comes walking up, and says, "Hey, man. I watched this movie, you know, and I can't think of it, but it's about this girl. And she turns into something. And she starts killing people."

"Okay," I say.

And he, with the most obnoxious swagger and utmost confidence, touches his nose a couple of times and looks to the side. Then he says, "Yo, you know? I remember what it was. You know, it's that movie *Speck-Ease*."

In utter disgust, disdain, and disappointment, I look at the gentle-man and say, "Sir, do you mean *Species?*"

Without missing a beat, he says, "Oh, yeah, yeah. *Species.*"

That's when I decided that I wasn't going to do that for another day. I told myself, *Hey, I have a very limited amount of time to get this thing done. And if I don't do it right now, I'm never going to do it.*

It was time to go become a Navy SEAL.

3

PASSING THE SEAL TEST

The very next day, I went to the Navy recruiter in Dayton, Ohio, and signed up for the Navy. It was July 1996, and I had dropped out of college. After that sobering conversation in the video store, I knew I couldn't stay where I was. I wasn't satisfied with mediocrity. I wanted more.

I was ready to finally start my journey to becoming a Navy SEAL. Everything came flooding back … the conversation with Jeff, the video that I saw, the determination and drive I felt, and the obsession I had with achieving this goal. I knew it was time.

I shipped out with the Navy, and what came next was totally unexpected and a little humbling, but definitely what I needed to get back on track. I didn't realize the difficulty of what I was about to do or how unprepared I was for the work that was necessary to achieve my goal.

I was in Great Lakes, Illinois, at Navy Boot Camp on ship number seven. It became apparent as we were getting our uniforms that I didn't do research about the Navy. I didn't even know what the uniforms looked like.

All I knew was there were ships that I didn't want to be on and long deployments—yet another thing I didn't want to be on. I also knew that Boot Camp was eight weeks, and I knew that I was going to trade school to be a Mineman (a Navy Source Rating or profession in the Navy where you detect and neutralize underwater mines).

But other than that, I knew nothing.

So I show up, and they're passing out uniforms. They hand me these blue jeans with bell bottoms. Awful. Then they hand me an equally awful blue shirt. And they say, "Alright, here's your uniform. Next."

I stopped the gentleman. "No, sir. I don't think you understand. I need a Navy SEAL uniform."

He looked at me and said, "Son, do you even know how to swim?"

I looked back at him like, *Why wouldn't I know how to swim?* And instantly I knew that he was really saying.

Look, you're black, man. I know you don't know how to swim, and you're not going to make it through the SEAL Teams. You're barely going to make it through the Navy portion of the test.

And from that point on, I mentally took that guy's name down and thought, *You know what? I'm gonna come back here in my uniform, and I'm gonna make you respect me.*

So I went through the first couple of weeks of boot camp. The homesickness, transitioning from Blockbuster to this four-year commitment in the Navy, getting yelled at, and trying to figure out what the Navy was about—it was all proving to be much harder than I had anticipated.

In the first week, we sat through the video of Naval Special Warfare, and Steve Brown was our instructor. He was this wiry guy with a mustache and the first Navy SEAL I'd ever seen in real life. As he described what our Navy career would be like in the unlikely event that any of us made it through the test, let alone BUD/S, somehow his presence gave me a boost of confidence that I hadn't felt before.

I was still as enthusiastic about the video, which was an updated version of the one I had already seen, but unlike the million other times I had watched it, this time was different. *This time*, there was an actual Navy SEAL talking about the SEAL Teams.

Now that I was one test away from the first step in my journey, I felt that familiar spark again. At that moment, I knew I was in the right place.

Our instructor told us what the SEAL Teams were, about the deployments, how hard the training was, and the attrition rate. None of that was a deterrent. I was super excited and decided to refocus because I was ready to be there.

The adjustment stress of the first couple of days of boot camp was starting to wear off, and I was getting into a routine. Instructor Brown said, "If you guys are interested, during week four, you can take the physical fitness test, which is a series of push-ups, pull-ups, a one-and-a-half-mile run, and a 500-meter swim."

Week four shows up, and I'm ready. I'm pretty nervous because I know I'm gonna have a problem with the pull-ups. But there were only eight pull-ups, and I had been a college athlete, so I thought I'd prepared myself for going into the Navy and taking the test.

But the day came, and I had never done everything in sequence.

I did the swim. Passed the swim. Did the push-ups. No problem with the push-ups. Did the sit-ups. No problem with the sit-ups.

And then came the pull-ups.

As I said, I hadn't prepped for doing the pull-ups, and I hadn't really done any pull-ups in my life. I just thought that if I was strong in every other aspect, then doing the pull-ups would be no big deal.

And to my embarrassment, I did two pull-ups. And they were the ugliest pull-ups you've ever seen. The instructors were baffled by how terrible my pull-ups were.

But they let me finish the test because even if I didn't pass, they wanted me to at least go through the entirety of the test. I passed the run because I was a gifted runner for my size. And I thought, *Wow, I embarrassed myself and showed that I wasn't actually quite ready for what I was getting myself into.* So I went back to lick my wounds.

I was a little discouraged because I thought I was going to do a lot better. But instead of letting my discouragement drag out, I was like, *Okay, what is the plan to succeed through this thing?*

I had to get better at pull-ups, but there were no pull-up bars available. Time was planned down to the minute during boot camp, so I needed a creative solution.

I noticed there was a bar over the toilet in the bathrooms, but it was metal and sharp. The first time I tried to use it, I almost cut my hands. It was around nine or ten each night after lights out, and I would go and do pull-ups for hours.

I had to improvise on how to do pull-ups without cutting my hands. The Navy does an excellent job of providing the basics during Boot Camp, and what I had plenty of were towels. As my solution, I put a towel over the sharp part of the bar and got to the business of getting better at pull-ups.

Just so you know, pull-ups don't get any better the more you do them when you're not good at them. Still, I would jump up and then slowly let myself down, and I was gradually getting stronger.

But I was up against a deadline, and I had to pass the next test in three weeks. If I didn't pass that test in three weeks, I was gonna go off into the Navy and just be a regular Navy guy. That couldn't happen.

The weeks passed, and each night I was doing pull-ups. Three days before the test, I had gone from two pull-ups to ten pull-ups.

It's important to note that for the SEAL test, you have to do *everything* perfectly.

Perfect form for push-ups. All the way up on the sit-ups. And when you did pull-ups, you had to get your chin all the way over the bar. It wasn't easy. But after several weeks of practice, I could do ten.

But I also knew that it was going to be ten pull-ups *after* going to the point of failure on push-ups and sit-ups. Not to mention, you're tired after the swim.

It was time for me to test again. I still passed the swim and did max effort on the push-ups and max effort on the sit-ups, so I felt pretty good. But I was still more tired than I had been just doing those bathroom pull-ups each night.

And then came the pull-ups.

I did one strong, two strong, three strong, four strong ... But I was starting to feel the fatigue. Five, got it. Six, got it. Seven, got it. But I had to take a little bit of a break. One more pull-up or my Navy SEAL dream was on hold.

I started going up for eight, I was 90% there, and through an act of God or karma or whatever it was, the instructor got distracted for half a second. I was like 95% there, but my chin wasn't over the bar. And as he looked away for that second, I told myself, *You're gonna have to do this thing, morals be damned. You have to get this last half-inch of a pull-up.*

As he looked away, I lifted my chin just over the bar and used my chin to pull myself all the way up. I hit eight, and the instructor looked at me and counted eight. But when he looked at me I could tell he was thinking, *You little bastard. I know you cheated. I know you cheated.* And it still counted as eight.

At that point, I knew that I passed, and I was euphoric. I was smiling at the bar. And the instructor said, "Don't smile. You still have a mile-and-a-half run left. And don't get cocky. You haven't passed yet."

But I was a runner, so I knew the run wasn't going to be a problem. We did the run, and I easily passed.

Then the instructor called, "Greene! Get over here!"

I said, "Yes, Instructor?"

He said, "Look, man, you're gonna have to work on your pull-ups. I know you cheated. I know you barely got yourself up when I looked around, but you know what? You got away with it. And I like your drive."

I didn't realize that the instructors knew I was doing pull-ups each night. But unbeknownst to me, my drill instructors had gone to the SEAL motivators, and said, "Hey, he's one of the best guys in the class. He's going to be a good sailor, but that kid's been doing pull-ups after hours for the last three weeks."

That meant a lot. The instructor had said that they talked to him on my behalf, and he was really rooting for me to do it. So when I actually did it, he said, "You have to take this test one more time at your A-School. So do me a favor, and work on those pull-ups. Everything else is good. You have a great work ethic. And we'll see you at BUD/S."

4

SURVIVING PRE-TRAINING

Pre-training for BUD/S wasn't what I expected. It wasn't something I could have prepared for because no one voluntarily works out at that level of intensity. When you're doing a two-hour morning physical training (PT), it is nonstop for two hours.

We never stopped moving.

Instructors were yelling at us.

And we were wet.

If we weren't doing our push-ups well or started struggling, they had us go into a rubber raft full of ice water.

Moving nonstop from one evolution to the next, we were exhausted, sore, and miserable. Sand was everywhere. And our bodies were in adjustment mode. We quickly learned that we were not fit enough to compete or do well when we got there.

We were definitely *not* in SEAL shape.

And remember, all of this was just *pre*-training.

Now, I consider myself a Type A-minus. I'm type A, sure, but I'm not anal or overpowering with my drive to succeed. You could say I'm a measured Type A. But you know, as a type A-minus, I really wanted to do well. I wasn't quite hitting the mark. *And I knew it.*

I was what's called "consciously incompetent," which means I was aware that I sucked and I knew I wasn't progressing as much as I thought. So I went to the instructor.

I said, "I'm not doing well. I thought I was going to be doing a lot better than I'm doing now."

"No, you're fine. BUD/S sucks. It's hard, and you're just getting here. Don't get discouraged. You're doing fine," he told me. "Now, get away from me because you smell like hell and you look even worse," he said with a slight smile.

But I was struggling, and I didn't believe him.

A few days later, we were headed into the weekend. I'd felt discouraged but was finally becoming encouraged because, by Thursday, I felt myself getting increasingly stronger. Friday was usually a lighter day, and then the weekend came.

By Monday, I was fully recovered. I was doing our daily PT (physical training), I was getting a few more push-ups, and I didn't feel as bad. I was able to do a few more sit-ups, hit a few more pull-ups, and swim longer. That's when I started thinking, *This isn't too bad.*

Then one day, it was hotter than normal. We had a couple of evolutions that were especially challenging, and after that, we had a four-mile soft sand run. Even though I was struggling, I knew I had gotten stronger and was feeling a lot better.

I was pushing really hard, and it was the last evolution of the day. Even though I had struggled with a few things, I was always strong in the running portion. We were running, and about three-quarters of the way through it, I knew something was wrong.

I was getting overheated, but I stopped sweating. I started looking around in somewhat of a panic because I didn't know if I was gonna make it.

We were running and running and running, and the instructors were yelling at us and trying to make us go as far as we could. I crossed the finish line, stumbled, got on my back, and the instructors were coming over.

It became obvious that I was in a really bad spot.

I could see that the instructors were yelling at me. And the scary part was that although I could tell they were talking to me, I couldn't understand them.

Words were coming out, but I just couldn't make out what they were saying. And I felt a solitary tear rolling down my face from my left eye because I was terrified knowing that they were speaking to me, but I couldn't understand them. I believed I was pretty bad off.

Of course, people fake injuries in an effort to get out of training or to try to get a break from training. So when they took me to medical, they took one look at me and said, "Oh, he looks like he's significantly messed up."

Finally, I reached the point where I could understand English again. The medics were studying my face like, *Mmhmm. This guy's fine. We got another one who's just acting like he's hurt.* So when it came time to take my temperature, they decided to see if I was faking it.

Rather than putting the thermometer under my tongue and getting my vitals, they thought, *You know what? We're gonna give this guy a rectal thermometer.*

Now normally, if you're faking, you don't want anything going in the "exit only," right? So you'd be very reluctant to get the probe. Well, they rolled me over, took my temperature, and I didn't move a muscle.

I *couldn't* move.

As they took my temperature, the entire medical staff was watching me. They all realized, *Oh man, this guy's not faking. He's really hurt.*

They put me on a medical hold. That means for twenty-four hours you're not allowed to do anything significant. So the instructor staff got in trouble for not making sure that we were hydrated throughout the day.

I went out to training the next day, and the instructor, Mike Getka, wasn't too happy. Mike was a great guy. He's a hardass, but a solid instructor. He'd received the brunt of punishment for not ensuring that his students remained safe during training.

He called me over and yelled at me. "Goddammit, Greene. You got me in trouble. So every time I see you, I'm going to tell you to go get your canteen. You're going to be hydrated inside and out. This means whenever I see you, you're going to be sure to drink all your water, and then you're going to go to the ocean to get wet."

The thing is, they only did that to students they especially liked and who they saw potential in. The truth is, Mike wanted me to get through it. That simple act got me through hell week and changed my mindset.

I listened to Mike. I got hydrated inside and out. I lived up to the SEAL ethos. I fought and survived until the end. I didn't quit. I didn't complain.

But after you miss a day of training, you feel like you let your team down. At that same time, I noticed a man named Senior Chief Mink who was a legend in the SEAL community.

He looked at me and said, "Hey, Greene. You know what? You're working really hard out there. I see you getting a little better every day. You asked instructors how to get better, you really want to be here, and I'm gonna give you a little secret."

He looked left, he looked right, lowered his voice, reached into his pocket, and he pulled out a bottle of sunscreen called Bullfrog.

Then he said, "Son, you're going to do great things here. I'm going to give you this thing of Bullfrog. Every student I've ever given this Bullfrog to has graduated, and I'm giving it to you because I know you're going to graduate. And if you tell anybody about this conversation, I'll deny it. But now you have this bottle of Bullfrog, and you're gonna make it."

I was 25 at the time. Here I am at more than twice that age, and I still have that bottle of Bullfrog.

The day I held that Bullfrog for the first time, I knew I was going to make it through BUD/S. It was life-changing. And it was the first time in my life up to that point that I had to dig so deep to succeed. That set the standard where I wouldn't accept anything less.

5

SUFFERING THROUGH HELL WEEK

There I was, getting ready to complete Hell Week. By the end of Wednesday, your body is such a mess that you're just there doing stuff to make sure that you'd survive it.

If you don't know what Hell Week is, it's the crucible event that all sailors must go through when they want to become a SEAL. It's five days, or 120 hours, of horrendous pain, suffering, hypothermia, delusion struggles, mental games, and everything else you can think of to torture somebody and bring them to the absolute brink of breaking … yet still continue.

Keep in mind, the attrition rate for Hell Week is usually around 60 to 70 percent, so it really weeds down the class.

It was Thursday, and we were going to finish Hell Week on Friday. We were in Boat Crew One. I was with Tim, George, Louis, Mike, and a couple of other guys whose names I can't remember.

We were in the middle of doing "around the world." The entire "around the world" challenge typically takes about twelve hours.

For the challenge, we took these little rafts that we'd trained with and paddled around throughout First Phase. First, we had to go north to one part of Coronado Island, then we turned back around and went several miles down the Silver Strand.

That part of the island is beautiful. With beaches, a country club, yachts, and palm trees, what's not to love? Well, we didn't see any of that shit while we were doing "Around the World." It was dark, wet, cold, and miserable—all normal conditions for Hell Week.

They have the whole thing nailed down to a science. It takes all night, and it's beyond grueling.

Traditionally, the guys in Boat Crew One are the biggest and strongest guys. We'd dominated every other event in Hell Week, and we knew it. By the time we got to this point, we were feeling a bit cocky and thought we'd be fine to cruise.

Needless to say, our boat was in last place, getting our asses kicked by everybody else. We were coming up on the end and pretty much not staying motivated or living up to our potential. Our instructors were livid because we were completely slacking, so they were yelling at us that we didn't even care.

The lead instructor had enough and said, "Hey, you guys better finish first. If you finish last … don't finish last," he warned. "And I tell you what, if you guys finish first, then you get to go to sleep until the last boat crew comes in."

Now, that could be a minute or that could be four hours, depending on how slow the longest guys take. In our minds, all we could think was, *Holy shit, we get to sleep.* To a group of sailors who hadn't slept in days, that motivation was exactly what we needed.

We poured it on. As we were going around the world, we started to hallucinate. We were paddling and paddling, and Tim started screaming uncontrollably and threw his paddle overboard. Of course, the rest of us were asking, "What the hell is going on?" Serious as can be, he said, "Throw your paddles away. All your paddles are snakes."

We all looked at our paddles and told him, "No, they're not snakes. They're just paddles." We turned our boat around, and we picked up his paddle. He was just in a really bad space. So we calmed him down and began rowing our boat again.

But then I started hallucinating. In the middle of the ocean, as plain as day, I see a fence. I was like, *Hmm. It's so weird to see a fence in the middle of the ocean.*

We had finally started to snap ourselves out of it, but everybody had already started to crash. Then, somewhere around thirty minutes later, I suddenly see a brick wall out there. And again, I was looking and thinking, *Wow, it's so strange to see a brick wall out here.*

Well, we'd drifted a little too far into the surf. So what I saw as a brick wall was actually a huge wave and our boat was headed straight for it. Sure enough, that wave overtook our boat and we were all thrown overboard. Paddles went everywhere. Our crew was scattered. Eventually, we got our bearings, gathered up, and went back to work.

We just kept going, we just kept paddling, and I'd say about four hours later, we reached the end in first place. *Rest, at last.* We stopped right there and crashed in the spot where we won when the instructors came up and said, "Hey, you guys. You guys won. Go get settled in."

We staged our boat and put it up on its side. We positioned the oars to make a lean-to, and we all snuggled in. All six grown-ass men. Snuggling.

When I say snuggling, I mean we couldn't have gotten any closer because staying warm was a priority. We hadn't been warm for the last four days. And just as I was settling in, instructor Getka called out, "Greene! Get over here!"

I immediately started cussing. "Ef this place, and ef that guy!"

I walked up to him, and he said, "Greene, remember when I told you that you're going to be hydrated inside and out?"

I said, "Yes, Instructor."

"Well, empty your canteen and go get wet," he told me.

It was like *The Return of the Jedi* when Darth Vader's supposed to kill his son. He looks at the Emperor, he looks back at Luke, he looks at the Emperor again, and then he throws the Emperor over.

You could say I had my very own Skywalker moment.

I looked over at Instructor Getka, I looked out at the water, I looked back at Instructor Getka, and I said, "Absolutely not. I will not go in that water."

That didn't go over too well.

Mike said, "What the hell did you just say?"

"I'm not going back in there."

He looked at me. "Say that one more time."

And with every bit of maturity I could muster, I threw a temper tantrum. Picture a full-grown man acting like a toddler in the grocery store. I was jumping up and down and stomping my feet.

I pretty much squawked at him, "You told me that we get to go to sleep. And we won, and I am not going in that effing water!"

Mike looked at me and said, "So are you quitting?"

I said, "No, I'm not quitting. You said I could go to sleep and goddammit, I'm going to sleep!"

In the midst of all of this, he called the chief over. The chief of that shift was a mean mo-fo and didn't mess around at all. Everyone feared the chief, and when the chief came over, you'd done something wrong.

Not only did the chief come but all the instructors followed him over, and the chief said, "What the hell's going on over here?"

And Instructor Getka said, "This guy is refusing to get wet."

Chief said, "Greene, what the hell's going on?"

I said, "Chief, Instructor Getka told me that once we finish, we get to go to sleep. We finished, and I am going to sleep because that's what he told me. And that's what I'm doing."

The instructors' faces said, *Oh shit. I haven't seen this before.*

And I remember this as clearly as it was yesterday. Chief looked over at Mike and said, "Mike, is that what you told him?"

"Yeah, Chief. That's what I told him," he answered.

Chief said, "We're SEALs. We keep our word. Greene, go back over and get some sleep."

I ran back into my boat yelling, "Tim, get ready! I'm coming back to bed!"

Tim was a mountain of a man at 6'4" and 240 pounds, and we were snuggled up like two infants.

I learned so much from that experience.

First, as a 25-year-old man, never throw a temper tantrum in front of other men.

Second, amid all the chaos and all the things you do in combat and special operations and SEAL Teams, being honorable is paramount.

Before this, "keeping your word" didn't hit home with me. It didn't have a meaning I could connect to. But after what the chief did, it struck a chord that no matter what's going on, what you say and keeping your word are the most important things.

The chief was mean, but he was a SEAL. To Instructor Getka, he basically said, "Nope, that's not how we do business. We keep our word around here."

And to me, he showed his honor by saying, "Hey, man, you got my word. You finished this first. Go to bed."

To this day, that's the best night of sleep I've ever gotten.

6

BECOMING A DAD

We were in the last couple of days of SEAL Qualification Training, or SQT, and we were all dirty and tired. We'd been out in the field for a week, and I kept looking at my pager, expecting the beeper to go off, but it never did.

(Depending on how old you are, you might not know what a pager is. It's a really, really old-school way of reaching people on the field when they didn't have a phone. It was issued to me for communication with my very pregnant wife. We had been married for ten months and baby number one was already on the way.)

One day, somewhere around 5:00 in the morning, this annoying beeping started. I was so tired that I didn't even recognize it was my own pager. I yelled out for the idiot with the pager, "Hey! Turn off that stupid beeper!"

One of the guys I was training with says, "Hey, stupid. That's *your* beeper."

Then it hit me. My wife had gone into labor and I needed to get all the way back to San Diego. To add to the stress, I think we were about eighty miles out. Everything that could go wrong went wrong.

There was a dedicated vehicle for me to take just in case. But in the middle of the night, somebody had a bug crawl in their ear and perforate their eardrum. So the vehicle that was set aside for me had already gone back to San Diego.

Here I was on this mountaintop with a pager going off, and I was freaking out because I was afraid that I might miss the birth of my daughter.

To give you some backstory on my daughter, she tested very high for potential birth defects. Her mom had to do an amniocentesis and a couple of other procedures to make sure that our baby was healthy.

Initially, she was thought to be a boy, and I was like, *Yes! Doesn't every father hope to get a boy at some point?* I was really excited about having a son. Yet when the results of the amniocentesis came back, my expectations shifted in an instant.

The emotions I felt were surprise and joy because the results also showed that our baby was completely normal and healthy and was going to be arriving on time. But what I wasn't prepared for was finding out our baby boy was actually a baby girl. I had no idea what to do with a baby girl.

Having a brother and boy cousins all over the place meant that dealing with a boy was going to be no problem. But dealing with a girl? I had absolutely no idea what I was doing.

So there I was in SQT with my pager going off in the middle of the night announcing the imminent birth of my baby girl, and because there were no vehicles in sight, I waited. And waited. And waited.

Six hours later, the vehicle came back, and I drove into Balboa Naval Hospital to find out where my wife was. She was still in labor and having complications. It was her first pregnancy, so neither one of us knew what to expect.

The nurse looked at the doctor and my wife, and they all saw the state I was in. I was covered in poison ivy, I hadn't showered in at least a week, and I was in no position to be in a hospital, let alone be in the room where my daughter was about to be born. So they sent me home.

I went home, showered, got cleaned up, and headed back to the hospital to wait. The next phase of getting ready for her birth was when the doctor came out and said, "Do you want to come see your daughter being born?"

And I said, "Hell yeah, I do!"

Looking back, I think it was a mistake because when you actually witness the birthing process, so many things go through your head …

You're amazed at how the human body can change so drastically when your wife is giving birth. Then you realize that she's getting ready to squeeze a watermelon through something the size of a lemon, and despite this painful reality, she's being told to push and push.

But then I saw my baby's head crowning, and I was mesmerized. And then the oddest thing happened. Her head popped out. She was just this little head—literally this little head, poking out and blinking. (You know, if my wife hadn't been looking at me, I would've probably screamed and run out of the hospital because it was such a strange sight.)

I put on my catcher's mitt and her shoulders popped out.

The doctor said, "Well, come on, Dad, pull her on out."

She came out, and she was the ugliest thing I'd ever seen. There was this white stuff on her, and she was skinny and pasty and seriously just atrocious.

But she was *my* little atrocious thing.

As soon as I held her, it was magic. She was finally in my arms, and for the briefest of moments, there were no worries. Then she started crying, and I knew that I was literally being a father.

Parenthood was upon both of us, and there was no turning back. And after about twelve hours, my baby girl looked more like herself and she was the most beautiful child. I was in love with the idea of being a father, but strangely detached from my daughter.

Now, what I had initially been told was, "This is a baby, and she's going to be wonderful, and you're going to bond with her right away." Unfortunately, I did *not* bond with her right away.

When you're a father, the baby doesn't need you all that much. And a lot of dads say things like, "I saw the baby, and she was just wonderful ... I fell in love instantly."

To me, that's a lie.

She was a crying, peeing, pooping machine that did not need me whatsoever. So I was just kind of bumbling around, and I didn't know what the hell I was doing.

I wasn't soft like her mom. I didn't have any milk. I was just this smelly thing that hurt her face with my prickly beard when I tried to kiss her.

Two months passed, and I was still trying to figure out how to bond with my daughter. I was doing what I could to foster an attachment, but as a father, I felt like I wasn't really necessary because she wasn't taking a bottle, so I couldn't feed her. I could hold her a little bit, but as far as bonding, I just didn't feel like we were connecting.

Still, every day, I came home from work and said, "Hi, Rylie."

She looked at me like, *Whatever*.

Until the best day.

She was about three months old. I came home from work and greeted her like I always did. I just called her name.

"Hi, Rylie."

And this time she looked up and smiled. I was just standing there thinking, *Well, what the hell is that?*

And I popped my head back around the corner, then came back and said, "Hey, Rylie."

And she looked at me and smiled again.

I was like, *Nah, this can't be happening.*

So, I did it for the third time. And she smiled.

That's when I realized, *She knows who I am.*

From that point on, I was absolutely smitten. One smile from this three-month-old little thing completely melted me all the way down to my soul.

7

DISCOVERING I'M A SEAL, NOT A SUPERHERO

Hell Week came and went, and thirty-six of us survived, which is a really good number. Our minds and bodies were pushed to their limits, so after Hell Week, we weren't permitted to go in the water. We weren't even allowed to get wet because we were basically hydrophobic.

We'd been in the water for countless hours. And being uncomfortable in the water for that long gave us all some type of PTSD. We had to stay out of the water and slow down our pace. It wasn't a big change, but just enough for us to heal before we started up again at the same grueling pace as the previous five weeks.

But we still had to get things done. We still had our morning PT.

We had to walk everywhere. Our feet were a mess and our hands were a mess. We had to do our PT, and then there were a bunch of classes and stuff. That time was essentially designed because they recognized what we'd just been through. We'd made it over a giant hurdle. So we were allowed recovery time.

As I was recovering, I struggled with disappointment because I didn't feel any different. I thought I was going to open up my shirt and find a big red S on my chest. I'd have a cape. I'd be able to fly around like a superhero.

Despite that, I felt exactly the same as I did when I got my Bullfrog, and I knew I was going to make it. Yes, I felt *exactly the same* after going through what's legendarily hard.

As I was going through the week, I fell into somewhat of a depression because I'd dug really deep and put in all this work. I'd done something that very few people can survive, I made it, did really well … and I felt the same.

Normally, I was laughing and very upbeat and just happy, but my lack of superhero-ish feelings was getting to me. I was walking up to my instructor John Cunning, and he said, "Hey, Greene, what's the matter?"

"Well, I'm struggling. I'm having a really hard time after Hell Week because I don't feel any different," I said.

"Hey, Greene. Have a seat, and let me tell you something," he said, and I sat down.

"I know how you feel because I felt the same way when I finished that week. You've been through Hell Week, and you know it's something that we all have to go through. So, what's the problem?"

I said, "You know, Instructor, I don't feel any different."

He very calmly said, "Yeah, you're not going to feel any different."

And I said, "What do you mean?"

"You have been a SEAL your whole life … Your upbringing, what your parents did—however you got here—you've been this your whole life. The secret of BUD/S is that BUD/S is not here for guys like you. BUD/S is for the people who aren't SEALs."

Naturally, I looked up and said, "So, I've always been this awesome?"

He broke character, laughed, and said, "Yes, Greene, you've always been this awesome."

Getting through Hell Week was just part of the process for me to know who I really am. It's who I've always been, and no matter what came of Hell Week, no matter how hard it was, I was always going to make it.

That was one of the things that I had never really thought of. I just thought I would feel different, that I was supposed to feel different. But I never did.

My journey through BUD/S served to shift my perspective. It was changing impenetrable barriers into surmountable obstacles, looking at a problem, and using teamwork or ingenuity to solve it.

Once you mentally shift the problem to becoming an obstacle, you may have to do some things to negotiate it, climb above it, go around, or go below it. But it's not something that's seen as a deterrent any longer. It's just something you have to work through and survive and outsmart.

And then you get to move on.

That's exactly what Hell Week was. It was the selection process of BUD/S. And it's changing your mindset and having an on/off switch of high intensity under the most arduous conditions that require you to think through them and survive.

You absolutely must persevere and dig deep every day and rely on your teammates to get through it. I already had all the attributes needed to be a SEAL. So, BUD/S wasn't built for me. It was for the 100+ guys who didn't make it because BUD/S had weeded them out.

I tell that story because when you are meant to do something or you're capable of, whether it's hard or easy, whether you get into Harvard or a junior college, whether you graduate or if you just do something that not a lot of people do ... you've had those attributes your entire life, and you just need to keep going through the process to be able to move forward.

I thought I was going to feel invincible after passing all the tests and pushing my mind and body to its limits during Hell Week. But I didn't. I didn't feel any type of personal transition, and that was very disappointing to me.

The same insecurities were still there. My mindset was still the same. My body had transitioned, but I couldn't recognize any mental transition. And I couldn't let go of my deep need to feel different.

It wasn't until my instructor told me, "You won't feel different. You've always been a SEAL. We just weeded out all the people who aren't SEALs," that it clicked.

I've always had the ability to overcome, thrive, and push myself to extremes.

After six months of grueling training and being selected for the SEAL community, I went through what's called SEAL qualification. I went from the basics that we learned in selection to learning what the actual job of being a Navy SEAL entails. It was another six months of rigorous training, but thankfully, it wasn't as arduous.

I was actually learning the job and doing things that I was going to need professionally in order to develop and excel as a SEAL. As I was beginning to establish myself in the community, I was also learning what it's like to be a husband and trying to figure out how to be a father.

One year into joining the Navy, I'd just graduated BUD/S, gotten married, and had our first child. We were newlyweds living in a new city in California, and the last thing I was prepared to do was be a father, but once Rylie arrived, there was no going back.

I had absolutely no idea what I was doing. I felt completely unprepared for all the change that was taking place at once and uncomfortable with the speed at which it was happening. Nothing about my old life was the same. Everything was different.

8

A NEAR-TRANSITION
TO THE AFTERLIFE

Transitioning from being single to being married ... transitioning from trying to *be* a SEAL to *learning about being* a SEAL ... and then transitioning from being a husband to being a father.

I was in transition overload.

Even though I still didn't know what I was doing as a parent and it took me a while to settle into being a dad, I had really bonded with my daughter.

Here I was, a full-fledged SEAL. I earned my trident. And I was about to be deployed.

As I was getting ready to leave, I had to say goodbye to Rylie. I asked her what she wanted to do, but I already knew the answer.

Rylie always wanted to go to the park. So, I put her in her favorite dress, got myself dressed up, and we went to the park. That was our official first date.

It was a normal Wednesday. And we had the best time … She was so much fun. She just went down the slide over and over, or I carried her, or I chased her. It was two precious hours of connecting and bonding with my daughter.

In those moments, I wasn't thinking about how our first date could easily have been our last. The line of work I was in reminded me often of my own mortality, but nothing could have prepared me for my first near-death experience.

If you've ever had a near-death experience, then you know they are life-changing. They shift your perspective and transform your appreciation for life and the small things that life brings. I've had multiple near-death experiences, and they've all been awful.

The first one happened during an exercise with a U.S.S. Kitty Hawk aircraft carrier. We were doing what's called visit, board, search, and seizure (VBSS), which means we get on the deck of a ship, take it over, render it safe, and turn it over to the Navy or Coast Guard who then take it to a safe harbor.

We were practicing on a boat called The Strong Texan. It was pretty small, so it was an incredibly challenging platform for a helicopter to put a SEAL Team on. The plan was to do what's called the Crawl, Walk, Run.

In Special Operations, we perform at the highest levels under some of the most challenging conditions on earth. However, we don't conduct any mission without a process of progressing to the point of expertise that's necessary for all of our missions. That's where the Crawl, Walk, Run method comes into play.

When we prepare, we do the basics of the mission (crawl) where we literally walk through and talk about the mission and answer any questions that the team has.

Secondly, we add more complex portions of the mission that include weapon systems, assets, communications, and an exercise that simulates the mission as closely as possible (walk).

Finally, the team puts everything together and we conduct the mission at full speed with as many complications as possible to simulate what the team will most likely see in a real-world mission (run).

During our exercise, we met with the pilots, got the briefing, took a tour of the helicopter where they would sit, and found out how the day's evolution would go. Next, we went out in the middle of the day for a practice mission when the seas were nice and calm. A helicopter came in, and we hovered over the platform, dropped off the assault team on Fast Ropes, and did a full-scale practice of the mission.

It was textbook.

But looking at the platform for the ship during the day … Well, there were cranes going everywhere, and there were a lot of obstacles on the ship. Those things mattered to getting the job done.

We met with a pilot—the annoyingly cocky pilot—and he happened to be the commanding officer of the HS-2. He came in very bravado, and said, "Okay, guys. I'm the best pilot in the squadron. I'm going to be leading this training exercise." (That attitude right there should've been a clue to his upcoming performance.)

Anyway, we got on the platform, and as I said, we executed beautifully in the morning. This was my first time, so I was thinking, *Wow, this is pretty cool.*

Then came the Night Evolution where we were actually doing the hit/assault on the ship. The nighttime was 100% opposite of the daytime. The sea state was very high, which means the waves on the ocean were dangerously close to the limit that would prevent us from executing because it was extremely dangerous.

Our helicopter circled the platform. The first helicopter sat on station, and the second helicopter held security. All those guys went down the rope, and they executed it perfectly.

But then the second pilot came in. He was understandably nervous, *and he should've been.* The entire profile of the mission was exceptionally tough. Shitty sea state, small platform on which to safely place sixteen SEALs, and the inexperience of the pilot made the entire night a perfect storm for something bad to happen. The ship was moving all over the place, making it much more difficult to stay on station and avoid the obstacles that were sticking thirty or forty feet off of the top of the ship.

Despite all of that, we had a job to do.

There were eight of us making our way down the rope. Number one went down, number two went down, and number three went down. Four, five, and six. There was only one other guy remaining and me, and the pilot was so nervous that he kept getting updates from the crew chief.

I heard him say, "One down, two down." The crew chief responds, "Hey, we have two more." And my teammate went down, leaving me as the last guy. So, I started making my way down the rope.

The gentleman in front of me hit the ground and got off the rope. Meanwhile, I was going down as fast as I could. But, the pilot thought the crew chief said there are no more guys. Suddenly, the helicopter started taking off.

I was leaving the ship. It wasn't fully registering with me what was happening. I looked down at the ship like, *Where's the ship going?*

All I could think to do was put on the brakes.

But I didn't really have anything to help me. I just had my hands to stop me, and I was weighed down with all my gear. I had my body armor. I had my boots. I had my weapon system. And they were all fully loaded, so I was *really* heavy.

Now, I was flying away from the ship—*out to sea*. I was headed down the rope, and I only had about two feet of rope remaining when I finally came to a stop.

As I looked down, I was trying to figure out how to climb back up this rope while flying through the air. I was almost to the point where I could climb far enough back up the rope to be able to stand on it and be relatively safe.

Of course, I knew how to climb a rope. It was part of training. They taught me how to climb rope when I was in BUD/S. It's something I did every day.

Keep in mind, I am a big guy already. I had extra weight from the gear. I had nothing to use as leverage under my feet. I was hanging there with only my upper body strength to move up on this rope ... and the rope is moving high above open water in the dark.

I looked up and a gust of wind hit the helicopter. I watched it buckle. That's when I could see that there was a whip that was moving fast down my rope, and I just looked at it. (If you've ever done battle ropes at the gym, you can imagine what this looked like. A wave of motion is traveling through the rope like a ripple.)

Oh shit.

I knew that it was going to snap me right off the rope. True to form, it snapped me right off, and I fell somewhere between sixty to one hundred feet into the water.

I wasn't prepared to be in the water, so when I landed in the water with a splash, I thought, *Why am I wet right now?*

None of it was making sense because this stuff wasn't supposed to happen. It put me in an ocean-soaked daze and possibly gave me a low-grade concussion. I hit the water—hard.

No amount of training can prepare you for the realities of SEAL Team missions until you're actually there.

The helicopter continued its leave. The waves were crashing on me, and the current was pushing me to the south. But the ship I should have been on was going north.

By the time the ship realized that I was overboard, the helicopter also realized I was overboard. But I wasn't close to either of them. I was drifting farther and farther away from the ship. To make matters worse, of course, everything that was supposed to work wasn't working.

I had a strobe light, so I turned it on. A strange sound came from the light as I turned it on, telling me that it leaked. Water got into the system and shorted out the light. Now I don't have that light.

Then my life vest failed—not because it didn't work, but because it's not rated to keep a 225-pound man with an additional thirty pounds of gear afloat. Yes. I was in the middle of the open ocean, weighted down, with no flotation device. It was dark, and I was alone.

In theory, the life vest was supposed to work. But it was rated for about 150 to 160 pounds. With all my gear on, I was about 100 pounds too heavy for it to hold me up.

I was starting to sink, and I had to tread water carrying all of that weight. To be clear ...

I had to tread water.

I had to keep my eyes on the ship.

I had to try to get my gear to work.

And I had to try to stay alive in a dark ocean.

The waves were crashing on top of me. I was literally sucking down so much water that it was burning my throat. In order to keep from drowning, I had to turn around and face away from the waves.

At that point, I kept getting pushed farther and farther out to sea. I turned on my headlamp. It was a bottom-of-the-barrel basic headlamp. It wasn't bright, and in the middle of the night in the Pacific Ocean, I might as well have been invisible.

Above me, I saw that the helicopter had started flying in a figure 8. It's how they do Search and Rescue. As the helicopter flew above me, I was about one hundred or two hundred feet outside of the figure 8 formation.

That means they couldn't see me.

The worst sound I've ever heard was that helicopter flying away from me in the middle of the night.

That's when I knew that I didn't have a chance of survival because the Pacific Ocean is vast. I was in no way prepared to be in 52-degree water for an extended amount of time. So I started to weigh my options. None of them were good, and my chances of getting back to my team or back to my family decreased every second I was in that frigid water.

How could I not panic? I believed I was about to die alone in the same waters where I'd been trained to be a friggin' badass Navy SEAL. Nothing about that was okay.

I quickly regained my senses and remembered the safety brief that they gave us ...

Well, the quarter that we were practicing in was off the coast of Southern California. It was between Catalina and San Clemente Island, which happened to be a great white breeding ground.

Oh. And it was mating season. (You can't make this up.)

There I was in the open Pacific, smack-dab in the middle of shark-infested waters, splashing around. All at once, I realized that I was getting ready to be shark food unless I calmed down.

I took a bunch of deep breaths and looked at my options.

I didn't know where I was. I didn't know if Catalina Island was north of where I was drifting or south. I was completely at a loss.

Fortunately, we had something on board that night that we weren't even supposed to have. We just so happened to get it at the last minute, and it was a night vision scope.

What I didn't know was that the pilot had picked up another SEAL from the boat. They lifted him up, and John was now a part of the search and rescue team.

The pilots couldn't see me, but finally, John had a bright idea. He thought, *I'm gonna try out this night-vision thing.*

Twenty or thirty minutes of treading water went by, and out of the blackness, I could hear the helicopter again. I heard it getting closer.

John had turned on the night vision. From about five or six miles away, my spare headlamp was just bright enough for him to see me. Imagine being spotted that far away from safety.

The best thing I'd ever heard was this helicopter coming toward me.

They were coming right toward me, and I knew that they'd seen me. It was just in the nick of time because I had started to get hypothermic, and I was teetering on the brink of death when the search and rescue diver came down to get me.

My circumstances were pointed directly to certain death. Sitting in that water, I was 100% positive that I was going to die. I was just waiting for death.

My body was reacting and had gone into full-on panic mode. And my mind was racing ... until it wasn't.

It felt like I was contemplating my death for an eternity before my training kicked in. Weeks and weeks of drills and training came flooding back.

My instructor was wrong, I thought. *I am a superhero.*

Although the rotors were kicking up so much water that I almost started drowning again and seriously contemplated staying in the water, that gray beast was the most beautiful sight I've ever seen.

The rotor wash was such a welcome feeling as the mist that they kicked up from my almost watery grave, confirmed that I was actually being rescued and it wasn't a figment of my imagination brought on by hypothermia and exhaustion.

The acrid smell of jet fuel and exhaust and the static electricity that the rotors generated all confirmed that I would live another day as a Navy SEAL. But it also confirmed that the platoon would lovingly give me so much shit for all the mayhem and chaos I caused.

One of the funniest things that I can remember from the experience is that the rescue swimmers had a script that opened with, "Hey, calm down. We're here to rescue you."

So, the swimmer splashed down in the water with his light buoy. Sure enough, he went to this script. "Hey, listen, calm down. We're here to rescue you. Are you okay?"

I looked at him and very calmly said, "Hey, man, I'm okay. Can you get me out of the water?"

He said, "Oh, well … Yeah, man. Let's get you out of the water."

They hoisted me up and rescued me. But I was uncontrollably shivering and possibly close to death. They wheeled me out covered in a heat blanket. In the middle of this emergency, several-thousand sailors were looking at me getting carted into the ship's infirmary.

And they had to cut my clothes off in front of everybody—*all of my clothes.*

Listen. I just want to go on record telling you that it was cold out. It was not representative in any way. And I hope I never run into any of those sailors that saw me in that state because it's not true. (I now have a much deeper appreciation for George Costanza changing his swim trunks.)

Back to the story.

I later discovered that all air operations were shut down because of my man overboard emergency. The helicopter went back to the Kitty Hawk. And they shut down all the F-18s launching that night.

As I was recovering, these two gentlemen came in and said, "Son. Son, what happened?" And I said, "You know, they shouldn't have had a pilot who didn't know what the hell he was doing! That guy almost killed me!"

The staff in the hospital, *everybody*—they all stiffened up. And they were all looking around like, *What did he just say?!*

So the gentleman said, "Alright, son. Well, I'm glad you're okay. And you take care of yourself."

Those two gentlemen walked out, and I asked, "Hey, who is the guy who just came back? I don't even know who that guy was."

They said, "Oh. That was the pilot who put you in the water."

And it was the HS-2 pilot. I don't know the commander's name, but it was aircraft number five and I will never ever forget that hull number.

What I learned from nearly dying (that time) is this: Your circumstances may be overwhelming and feel as if they will bury you. Do not panic. Go back to the truth of what you know for certain. Go back to your training. Go back to whatever grounds you. Lean into that, and let it lead you.

9

SURPRISED BY SNIPER SCHOOL

One day, I was casually walking on the training ground, enjoying the relief of being home with no immediate responsibilities. But that casual walk wouldn't last. I was jolted out of my relaxed state by someone aggressively approaching me. *What the hell?*

They asked what I was doing at that moment, and I confidently responded that I'd just returned from deployment and was going through my gear. To my total disbelief, they promptly ordered me to pack my things and prepare for sniper school because the team was meeting the next day and departure was scheduled for Wednesday.

I stood there, stunned, thinking it must be some kind of joke. It seemed inconceivable that someone could walk across the training ground and get selected for one of the toughest schools in the SEAL community, if not the entire military.

It's not like college. There isn't a club fair with people passing out flyers and bribing you with free T-shirts to join their group.

Nobody was recruiting us for professional development and certainly not for a highly specialized sniper training school.

You don't just *go* to sniper school. You can't just decide to show up and be a sniper. That is *not* how it works. And I definitely didn't expect it to work that way for me.

Eventually, I gathered my wits and began packing, still half-expecting to be told it was all a prank. I realized that if I'd been given this opportunity, I needed to take it seriously, even though I had no idea what sniper school entailed.

I didn't know the weapon systems, the training, or the challenges involved. All I knew was that the training lasted ten weeks, and it was famously grueling. Listening to others talk about it only intensified my intimidation.

Nevertheless, I showed up at the school with a smile on my face, ready to tackle the unknown. The instructor began explaining what we would be learning week by week.

The problem was, I didn't understand most of the terms he used. Concepts like the .300 Win Mag, shooting at distances of 1,000 yards, snaps, movers, and stalking were all foreign to me.

Meanwhile, I was surrounded by classmates who had waited years for this opportunity, while I had simply stumbled into it. I realized that I needed to make the most of it, so I sought out the experts in the class and bombarded them with questions, staying long hours after class to take in as much knowledge as possible.

I was determined to suppress my inherent twitchiness and learn to focus with precision—a skill that seemed counterintuitive to my natural inclinations. Twitchiness and being intensely focused didn't exactly go hand in hand.

During my sniper training, I found myself fully immersed in the pursuit of excellence. Each day, I meticulously tracked my targets, assessed distances, and considered atmospheric conditions such as humidity and elevation. My dedication to my newfound craft was unwavering, and I was relentless in my quest for success.

I made it my mission to push the instructor staff to the point where they had no choice but to tell me to take a break and return the next day. The challenge of it all was nothing short of exhilarating. I took the art of shooting very seriously.

Week after week, as people dropped out of the class, I remained steadfast. Even those who seemed more naturally talented than me didn't make it through. While the tests were incredibly difficult, I continued to work hard, improve my skills, and patiently eliminate any bad habits. I learned everything the right way, following the guidance of the best shooters in the military.

The shooting portion of the course spanned eight weeks, with an additional two weeks dedicated to stalking. My focus was primarily on the shooting segment, where I invested immense effort.

To pass the course, I needed to achieve a minimum of 80% on all the tests, and I just managed to meet that requirement. I secured a passing grade with a modest 80.2% on the shooting portion.

However, when we moved on to the stalking phase, which involved blending in with the surroundings using a ghillie suit and getting as close to the target as possible, I fell short. Fortunately, snipers were in high demand, and the instructors gave me the opportunity to retake the stalking portion.

I didn't let my initial failure discourage me. During the workup period, I sought guidance from qualified snipers in the platoon, absorbing every bit of knowledge they were willing to share.

When I took the course for the second time, the challenge was just as intense, and once again, I barely made it through. But I was determined to succeed.

It was time to transition from being a SEAL operator, a force that strikes swiftly and resets for direct action missions over and over, to becoming a sniper. Snipers are given a target and a timeframe in which to execute, which can range from a few hours to several days.

I had to completely shift my mindset and transform from a hammer into a scalpel. The work became precise, deliberate, and contrary to the SEAL Teams' approach of relying on surprise, overwhelming force, and violence of action to secure objectives.

The transformation was gradual, and I began seeing the world through a different lens. No longer did I perceive it as a vast open space; instead, I noticed the nuances, the details. I became attuned to the environment, feeling the wind and observing how it affected my shot. I learned to read the movements of leaves and decipher the behaviors of animals in the vicinity.

Awareness became paramount, not only of my own mind and body but also of everything happening around me. And the training encompassed not just sniping but also counter-sniping, as we had to assume that there was always another sniper lurking, hunting for us.

This experience was a complete shift, one that defied everything I'd learned in life up to that point. I had to discard my previous perceptions and approaches because if I made a mistake in this new realm, every decision, every action, every breath could be my last.

However, this was a transition I'd prepared for, so I embraced it wholeheartedly.

The lessons I learned during sniper school and my transition from enlisted to Petty Officer Third Class were invaluable. They weren't taught in a way that aligned with my preferred learning style, and that led to the opportunity to teach the sniper course myself.

It turned out to be the most rewarding experience of my military career. I took a group of young SEALs who were unfamiliar with the intricacies of sniping and guided them to become some of the best shooters in the world within the relatively short time frame of ten weeks.

As an instructor, I quickly realized that each student required individualized attention. Although they trained in pairs throughout the course, I had to adapt my teaching methods to accommodate their unique learning styles. What worked for one person might not work for another.

I invested considerable time and effort in understanding each student's mindset and tailoring my instruction accordingly. The joy I felt when my students no longer needed my constant guidance was immeasurable.

They would shout, "Hey, Mark, I got it!" on the same day they fired me as their instructor. That's when I transitioned from being a teacher to a mentor, providing course corrections and guidance as they grew more independent.

When I was first shoved onto the path of my sniper journey, I lacked confidence in myself. However, once I embraced the mindset of seeing it through, regardless of the challenges and the effort required, I emerged as a graduate of the course.

This experience shaped me into a well-rounded SEAL operator who could excel in direct action missions—the pit bull side of the job—as well as in the specialized (and often underappreciated) field of sniping.

If given the chance, I would undoubtedly choose to teach the sniper course again. Witnessing the transformation of my students, from novices to experts capable of operating downrange, was immensely gratifying.

I hoped they would return one day to pass on their knowledge to future snipers, just as I taught them. Similar to my experiences with OCS candidates and platoon members, I genuinely cared for my students and always sought what was best for them.

10

A PAIR OF SNIPERS TAKE SHOTS

Sniper teams do everything in pairs. We eat in pairs, we drink in pairs, we complain in pairs, and we do the job of sniping in pairs. One day my spotter, who we'll simply call "Salty," and I were selected to conduct a mission that, under ideal conditions, would have us take a shot from 800 yards (eight football fields) all the way out to a mile (eight minutes of continuous running for most of us).

Although all snipers are capable of taking long distance shots, the amount of preparation to be as sharp as possible on the battlefield takes almost superhuman preparation. Not only does it take preparation, but it takes ability, patience, and singular focus, no matter the environment.

For this particular mission, we weren't sure if we were going to take the shot at sea level, at an elevation of over 10,000 feet, in the desert, on a frozen tundra, from a vehicle, or from the traditional prone position. I tell you about all of those mission parameters because each scenario requires a different method of preparation.

All of the basics are the same, but the nuance is much, much different.

When I say nuance, I'm talking about the wind conditions at the target, the wind conditions halfway to the target, the wind conditions from your shooting position. Are there "indicators" that show you what the wind is doing? For example, if you're in the middle of a desert and there are no flags, trees, tumbleweeds, or anything to tell you what the wind is doing, then making the right wind call is exponentially more difficult.

In the world of snipers, the spotter is the better shooter of the pair, but he has the added talent of determining the wind conditions on an almost superhuman level. I was a good shooter and good at calling wind, but Salty was on another level. He just had a knack for it. But that knack required constant training and diligence as sniping is a perishable skill and at the distances we were tasked to prepare for, we both had to be at an elite level.

As the months progressed, we used the Crawl, Walk, Run method. We started from scratch, doing the very basics again. We progressed to a point where we could both take the shot and both call the right wind. We would sit near a clearing just paying attention to the rhythm of nature. How bugs move, how the wind changes direction, how the humidity changes, and the seemingly endless variables that we're going to face once we're on target, which could be a mile away.

Please take a moment to imagine how far that is … I'll wait.

The days turn into weeks that bleed into months, and Salty and I are almost ready. We barely talk anymore because we're so in tune with each other. Normally there is a lot of chatter between shooter and spotter that, if not handled the right way, could give away your position and ruin the entire mission days or weeks before you're supposed to take the shot.

By now we're speaking to each other in a series of guttural grunts, head nods, or the slightest body movements that communicate volumes that most people would never pick up on.

One day, we decided to take a break and do some plinking with our .22 rifles. As Salty and I were shooting the same hole of our target so many times, a beautiful circle emerged where the center of the target used to be. And of course we were bored.

Then, something changed. I didn't see that Salty got excited, but I could somehow feel it, so I got on my scope to see what he was seeing. I couldn't quite see what he was looking at, but he kept saying, "Don't move, fucker."

I looked at the barrel of his gun starting at the scope and slowly traced my way to the tip of the barrel. Once I figured out where he was looking and calculated that his rifle was accurate out to about 25 yards, I saw it. There was a fly buzzing around. Salty's new target.

When you're as tuned in to the environment as we were, you never aim for the target. You aim for its final destination. Salty predicted where the fly would land and was holding his crosshairs on that spot instead of chasing the fly around.

I looked through my scope, and just as I put my crosshairs on the predicted target, I heard the familiar report from his rifle that the .22 projectile was breaking the sound barrier on its way to the target.

I saw that fly vaporize and was impressed. It was an amazing shot!

Not to be outdone, I started looking for my own fly, but there were none to be found. Like any good sniper, I started looking for a different target. I had to get something, or Salty's shit-talking would never stop, and I couldn't have that. After about five minutes, there it was.

A bee was buzzing around, and as I tracked him, I started looking around for a flower, any flower that would be a likely place for my target to land. Out of the corner of my scope, I saw a pristine flower that I would definitely check out if I were a bee.

I put my crosshairs on the flower and waited. As predicted, the bee came closer and closer until it found its target, and as soon as it landed, my rifle coughed, and another .22 missile was heading at full speed to my target.

In an instant, my target vaporized, and I very smugly looked over at Salty and said, "That was a pretty good shot, wasn't it?"

He said, "Yep. But it wasn't as good as hitting a fly." Then he let out this evil laugh.

I was pissed because I knew he was right, and I officially lost our impromptu shooting contest.

We were a week away from inserting for our mission, and this was the most difficult week because not only did we have to confirm and reconfirm our D.O.P.E. (Data of Previous Engagement), but we also had to calculate the Coriolis Effect.

In basic terms, it's how the rotation of the earth affects the round at extreme distances and since we were preparing to shoot out to a mile, we had to calculate for this effect on the round.

The moment of truth was upon us. We saw the target, but it was so far away—so far, in fact, that we had to hold our crosshairs an entire football field to the right of the target, just so the wind would push the round onto the target at such an extreme distance.

Let me try to describe how this feels ...

Do you remember when you went on your first date with the person that you've had a crush on for a while? The butterflies are turning your stomach in ways you didn't think possible.

Your hands start to sweat, and you momentarily forget how to use the English language. You have this reaction even though you see this person all the time and admire them from afar. But you've hyped yourself up to ask them out for the longest time, and to your surprise, they say yes.

You go to pick them up, ring the doorbell, and wait an eternity for the door to open. You debate whether to run away before the door opens and make up an excuse later.

The moment passes, and you're graced with the vision of your date. You realize that everything is going to be ok. You've prepared for this moment, and although you're nervous, you realize that you're about to go on the perfect date.

That's how it feels when your real target comes into view. You have that "*oh shit*" moment and then settle back down and wait for the familiar sounds of your spotter.

As Salty continuously calls out the wind conditions and where to hold my crosshairs, I hear what I've waited for over a year to hear:

"Take the shot."

With two and a half pounds of pressure on the trigger, I unleash all the discipline, dedication, persistence, patience, and drive for excellence that have culminated in this moment and think to myself, *I love this shit and hope I can do this for the rest of my life.*

11

THE PASSING OF A WARRIOR

When you're doing this very dangerous job of special operations, you are inevitably going to lose people. What we do is hard. Training real-world missions is hard. We train as realistically as possible. And with that training, you're going to lose people.

I lost an incredible friend.

His name was Mike. We'd been through BUD/S together. We were great friends, and our kids were born at the same time. Our time was spent constantly hanging at each other's houses. And even our wives were good friends.

It happened after sniper school.

We'd finished our first deployment, we'd gone through ten weeks of sniper school, and we were exhausted. Mike just graduated and had a very short time to go to what's called "freefall." It was skydiving, also known as military freefall.

He was at my house on a Sunday, and was shipping out that Monday to go skydiving. He was a couple of days late getting registered, so he wasn't supposed to be able to go. But they gave him a waiver so he could attend.

We were having a get-together. The two of us were hanging out when he said, "Mark, I'm just tired. I don't really want to go into freefall. But you know, these billets don't come very often."

He was torn as to whether he was going to take it or not.

I looked at Mike and said, "There's no reason to go. You're the golden child around here. You're gonna get another opportunity. Why don't you just stay home?"

But staying home wasn't in Michael's DNA. He decided he wanted to go. So Mike headed off that Monday to go to his military freefall course.

And that's the last time I saw him.

For me, it was life as usual. We were back at the team, getting ready to start training again, and we were called into a meeting on Wednesday. They called the entire command onto the grinder and said, "Hey, we have an announcement. There was a fatality—"

Michael had died in a parachuting accident.

As the commanding officer told us about Michael's tragic death, the level of shock I felt was so overwhelming that I can't even describe it to this day.

We went back into our platoon space and waited. That's when the Commanding Officer showed up at our platoon hut. You see, the military does death notification in a very specific way, so they were making plans.

As soon as he walked in, he said, "Hey, I need to speak with Mark."

He spoke to me privately. "Mark, I need you to do something incredibly important. Michael's wife and new son had to go to the hospital. The car's broken down, and you need to go pick them up at the hospital."

I said the only thing I could. "Okay."

But then he said, "You cannot tell his wife that Michael has died. And I know it's gonna be hard, but I know it's something you can do. So grab your stuff. Go get in the car, and go pick up his wife and son, and take them home."

I drove up to Balboa Naval Hospital and saw Mike's wife and child. His wife got in the car, and the hardest thing I've ever done was to look her in the eye knowing her husband's dead, *and I couldn't tell her.*

The drive home was about thirty minutes, and she was talking about Michael's freefall class and how he calls her each night to talk to her and their son. She was pretty excited about it and said, "He just loves it, but he's going to be home this weekend."

My gut was churning, and my insides were a mess. That man was family to me. I had to sit there and play along like I didn't know he was gone. Like I had no idea that her heart was about to be shattered.

This is the point where a typical person would cry. I experienced all the signs that my body needed to release the grief, sorrow, and anger that I was feeling. My heart was racing, my chest felt like it was locked in the world's biggest vice grip, and there was a lump in my throat that stole my ability to speak. What I really needed to do was express sorrow through tears, but the tears never came.

Although I was not in the SEAL Teams for very long, the ability to connect to emotions had been replaced by cold logic and the constant cycling of my brain to fix the problem. I figured I would get around to crying at some point, but for now, I had to stay focused on remaining stoic and express the only acceptable emotion that I had available—outright anger.

I dropped her off at the house and went back to work. I was still very much in the midst of processing the tragedy, and I felt like such a scumbag because I had to keep it from her. I knew her entire life and the life of her son were going to change.

The Commanding Officer, the Chaplain, and the Command Master Chief put on their dress uniforms and showed up at the house to tell her that Michael had died.

It was a very small community, and everybody descended on the house with their condolences. As I walked through the door, Mike's wife, now a widow, looked at me in a way that I will never ever forget.

She glared. *You motherfucker. You knew that he was dead. You let me think he was still alive, and you betrayed me by not even telling me.*

Losing one of my best friends and the trust of his wife was devastating. And even though I was following orders, I'm still human. My feelings were *and are* still there. To this day, I don't know if she's ever forgiven me for that.

I cared for Michael deeply. He was a phenomenal guy, an exceptional teammate, and a remarkable father. He was taken away from us too soon.

It has taken me years to try to get back to normal. We had been through so many seemingly impossible things together, and I haven't been the same since losing Michael on July 12, 2000.

On the same day that he passed, there was an instrumental song playing called "Rock Your Baby" by KC and the Sunshine Band. I had it on repeat because I needed something to keep my mind off of the pain. To this day, every year on July 12, I play that song on repeat.

Even as I tell this story, it's still very emotional and hard to deal with. I still feel the loss. I haven't seen Michael's wife or son since then, and hopefully, she'll read this book and know that I'm sorry that I had to deceive her. That experience changed my life.

And it'll be with me until the day I die.

12

THE INVISIBLE HAND

When I first joined the SEAL Teams, I was *not* looking forward to combat per se, but I knew it was a very real possibility. Tip-of-the-spear type things could happen. You go through this selection process to become the best of the best, and with that comes the knowledge that you're going to be on the front lines of everything combat related.

At the time, we hadn't experienced a real war conflict since Vietnam. Nevertheless, we trained at a very high level, always ready to go. But oftentimes, there was no real-world mission to go on. Then, 9/11 happened, and my platoon was deployed to Okinawa, standing by to support the fleet and their wartime mission planning.

When September 11 happened, I was suddenly forced into a major life change. Peacetime was over, war was on, and we got the call to join the U.S.S. Germantown. We were steaming toward Jakarta because Indonesia had the highest Muslim population outside of the Middle East and the US Embassy was under threat of attack.

As a Battlegroup, we were preparing to go and were on board the ship. The missions we had planned were very sensitive, which required us to be isolated from everyone.

The regular Navy didn't want SEALs to pollute their sailors because our presence along with what we do was completely at odds with the Navy's mission. (It's basically an oil and water mixture.) But they were very accommodating because we were part of their mission.

And as we were training, we had to figure out how to do our missions on this craft that we'd never been on. It wasn't configured for us, and we had to make some modifications to how we do business.

One day, we were out in the middle of the ocean, and they announced that they were having special operations practice. Everybody else was on the fantail of the ship because they'd heard the SEALs were on board and they'd never seen us.

The adrenaline was running really high because we were preparing to do what we trained so hard for. But death was always around the corner. And somehow death seemed to be chasing me down … *again.*

We were getting ready to get back on board the ship, so they flooded the deck as we brought our zodiac in. All eyes were on us, and we had a couple of new guys on our team, along with the spectacle of all the sailors.

We had to prepare to jump off the boat quickly—as soon as we hit the flooded deck of the ship. As we came up on our final approach, we were approaching in a straight line. And one of the new guys was steering the boat.

That new guy just kind of looked up, marveling at the audience watching us. That was when he started to veer off to the left. I was on the left side of the boat, so we yelled, "Hey, you're off course!"

Being a new guy, he overcorrected when we were about twenty or thirty feet from the fantail. In a blink, the boat jerked, and I fell into the water. I was immediately caught up and pulled into the prop wash.

At first, I was at the water's surface near the props. And those props are huge. They were turning up a lot of water. Within that churn, it was almost like a giant vacuum.

Well … I *was* on the surface of the water.

Before I knew it, I was at least thirty feet under the water. I couldn't see the propellers, but I could see all the water getting churned up. I tried to swim to the surface, and it was as if a huge hand was holding me down.

I couldn't move.

And yet, I wasn't panicking.

I think it was one of the calmest moments I've ever had. I literally sat still, leaned back in the water, crossed my legs, and crossed my arms as if sitting in a lounge chair thirty feet underwater. I was just looking up. I couldn't believe this was happening again. And like the first near-death story, I had my life preserver and knew I was getting ready to pop it.

I could've shot up to the surface, but I didn't know what was up there. I didn't want to pull my life vest and end up underneath the ship or somehow in the prop.

So I was just leaning back. I continued to hold my breath and felt my anger skyrocket with every moment that I was trapped under that ship. I was irate at the kid who put me in the water.

Then, I tried to swim up again. *Nothing.* That invisible hand wasn't moving.

All I could do was sit there and think, *Man, if I die down here, I'm going to be so pissed.* I looked down at my life vest again, and I thought, *If I pop this thing, the guys are gonna give me so much shit. I'm never gonna live it down.*

As I was looking down, considering my options, I felt myself starting to float up a little bit. So I said to myself, *Alright, Mark. Give it one more try. And if you can't get up on this try, then go ahead and pop it.*

I started to swim up, and it was taking a while. Finally, I reached the surface and I couldn't believe how far away the ship was. Our ship was a *quarter mile* from where I landed in the water.

When you're walking or driving, 400 yards doesn't seem too far. For swimming, it's four laps in a pool. Four laps in a pool after being held under and then fighting your way to the surface? That ship felt very far away.

Even at a distance, I could tell the ship was going crazy because they had a man overboard. It was the same thing as the last time I nearly died. And before any other thoughts, I was like, *I'm going to kill the kid who dumped me in the water.*

Again. Looking back, it wasn't the same kid, but the same situation. There I was, thirty feet down in the middle of the ocean. More than likely, there were sharks everywhere around me, and I was on the verge of losing my life.

Yet somehow it was the calmest I'd ever been.

Once they spotted me, my platoon hopped back in their boats and headed out to get me. They couldn't believe that I survived because once they realized the literal gravity of it, they thought, *Yeah, he's dead.*

A couple of my teammates who were with me the other time I had my near-death experience pulled me out of the water, and they said to me, "Mark, you might need to get into a different line of work because this whole water thing is not is not your jam."

My eyes screamed, *Go FUCK yourself.* But as my hand reached for his extended hand, my body language radiated, *Thanks for coming to save my ass again.*

It turns out that I was underwater for over two excruciatingly long minutes. I only had one breath to prepare to go into the water, and when I hit the water, I immediately sank.

Even today, I can't explain what happened. I don't even know if my training kicked in. But I survived it.

I figured I had three strikes. So in my head, I was keeping count. I thought, *Okay, I had the first one. And then I had my second one. The third will be the strike out of my life. The next one will be my last one.*

That's a story for another time.

13

DOUBLE INTERVIEW
WITH ADMIRAL STOCKDALE

I'd been on the SEAL Team for four years. During that time, after my first platoon and in the middle of our second deployment, I managed to finish my bachelor's degree.

I had an amazing experience during my first deployment. The leadership and the dynamics of the platoon were strong, and I learned a lot. So, I decided to talk to my Officer in Charge (OIC) about the possibility of becoming an officer someday.

He said, "Mark, I don't recommend you go after this deployment; I recommend you go after another one. The dynamics of the platoon are really in line with how things are supposed to go. You're going to learn more from bad experiences or leadership challenges or teammate challenges and command challenges than you will from this one. As far as a picture-perfect workup, deployment, and team dynamics, this is a really good example."

I respected his counsel. Plus, I knew I had another deployment to do, so I wasn't quite eligible. OCS would have to wait.

Then I had my second platoon, and his words proved to be true. The dynamics were different. The leadership style was different. And I was learning a lot from the lack of experience.

My previous Chief Petty Officer (CPO) had been in for a long time, and my OIC was prior enlisted. They understood how to manage a SEAL platoon throughout the workup cycle and deployment.

In my second platoon, we were all much younger, and a lot more mistakes were made. In light of that, I felt that it was time to transition from being an enlisted SEAL to becoming a SEAL officer.

At the time, you had to be a certain age to become an officer, and I was close to exceeding that age limit. But all the stars must've aligned because in the six or eight months before my second deployment, the Navy changed the age waiver. It went from 28 to 34.

After that deployment, I said to myself, *Well, you know what? I'm going to give this thing a try because I feel like I'm qualified. I think I'm smart enough to do it.* I wanted to transition from taking orders to being a facilitator and the challenge that came with achieving that goal.

So, I was at a Fourth of July party and this gentleman there heard that I wanted to become an officer. He was a WWII veteran named Dean Laird. Laird was the only fighter ace in the Pacific Theater *and* the European Theater. And he was also a legend in the aviation community as well as the Navy community.

While I was at the party, I said, "Mr. Laird, I believe that you know I'm trying to become an officer. When I told my commanding officer that I want to become an officer, he said, 'You have to go as high as you can go, reach for the stars because you're going to need a really strong recommendation.'"

I thought it was perfect because I had access to a legendary fighter ace. Having him write a letter of recommendation would've been an amazing accomplishment.

While I was talking to Mr. Laird, he said, "Son, you know what, I'm not a great writer, and I'm not really good at that stuff. But I have a really good friend who I think would love to at least have an interview with you."

And I said, "Yes, sir. Okay."

"Give me a call in a couple of weeks. I have to go do some things," he said.

Mr. Laird must have been close to 80, and I thought, *This guy's not going to remember me at all.* But I was determined. I had a course of action. And now, I had a plan.

Several weeks passed, and I gave Mr. Laird a call. He said, "Son, I remember, and I talked to my friend, and he would love to meet you. Jim is going to have you give him a call, and he'll set up a meeting with you."

And as I said, "Sir, I am sorry, but I don't know who Jim is—"

He interrupted. "It's Admiral Jim Stockdale."

We'd gone through survival training, and Stockdale's experience had provided a significant portion of that training. He won the

Medal of Honor. He was a vice-presidential candidate, a Naval Academy grad, and an all-around legendary guy.

Naturally, I started to freak out.

I said, "I'm not prepared to talk to an admiral. I was just gonna talk to you or a captain or something."

"No, he's already agreed to it. So, get dressed up and give him a call," he told me.

When I called Admiral Stockdale, he said, "Young man, come on over. I'd love to have you come over and talk this OCS thing all the way through."

I said, "Sir, just so you know, my grades in college weren't the best because—"

"I don't wanna hear about that shit. I want to hear what you've accomplished. And I don't care about your grades. I've asked around about you, and people speak really highly of you. So you come on over and we're gonna have this *now*."

You just don't argue with someone as decorated as Admiral James Stockdale. So I showed up to Mr. Stockdale's in my dress uniform, and he said, "Son, come on in."

He was the absolute nicest gentleman I'd ever met, just a sweetheart of a guy, and he took me on a tour of his house. We sat and had a beautiful interview. We were just having a conversation as he asked me a series of questions.

"Son, we're gonna get you in to be an officer. I guarantee it," he said.

I replied, "Yes, sir."

But the next day, I got a phone call from Mr. Stockdale and he said, "Son, where the hell are you?"

What I didn't know at the time was that he'd started to suffer from dementia. He'd forgotten that I'd been there the day before. Dutifully, I said, "Yes, sir. I'm on my way."

I got dressed again. I went to his house and had a mirror of the same interview that day. I was happy to do it because he was such a lovely man. Just being around him and hearing some of his stories was really valuable to me.

A couple of weeks passed, and I gave him a call, and said, "Admiral, they're still waiting. I haven't heard back from the command."

Without missing a beat, he fired, "That's bullshit. Alright. I've had enough. Alright. Give me a call back later on today."

"Yes, sir."

He went straight to the Naval Special Warfare Command (WARCOM), showed up at the quarterdeck, and said, "Who the hell do I have to screw around here to get Petty Officer Greene in OCS?!"

You know those scenes in movies where papers are flying? It was like that. And I mean, things were going crazy.

The Executive Officer said, "Who the hell is Petty Officer Greene?"

Pandemonium happened, and two weeks later, they told me, "You are good to proceed with your Officer Candidate School package."

Stockdale said, "Now, Mark, I've got something to talk to you about. When you go see Johnny, you tell him that you and I talked, and tell him you hang with the big boys now. He'll know exactly what you mean." He gave me a wink, a firm handshake, and told me to do my best.

Before I walked away for what was the last time I'd ever see Admiral James Bond Stockdale, I let him know that I didn't know who Johnny was. "I'm talking about Johnny McCain." The look in Admiral Stockdale's eyes when he mentioned "Johnny" was a look of genuine joy at the thought of his very dear friend.

Unfortunately, I never got a chance to get on Senator McCain's schedule before he passed.

That was a lesson in gratitude and humility that has stuck with me because this man had been through so much. Still, he'd taken the time to make sure that I was set up to succeed as an officer.

He wrote this handwritten letter that I still have (check the photo gallery at the end if you want to see it).

Admiral Stockdale changed my life with that experience. It was a mission I couldn't accomplish on my own. He was in the military stratosphere and accomplished so much while a prisoner of war.

His heroism, dedication, and actions at the Hanoi Hilton are now memorialized in Survival, Evasion, Resistance, and Escape (S.E.R.E.). The man was a true legend, and I had the honor of spending two days with him. It's still one of my favorite stories to tell (but it also came with some caveats, which I'll discuss later).

14

AVOIDING SABOTAGE

The SEAL Teams are a slice of the U.S. You have rich, you have poor. You have tolerant, you have intolerant. So when I started the transition from enlisted military to officer as a black man in a community that is over 90% white, I faced a different type of challenge.

I went from *taking* orders to being in a position of *giving* orders and having people's lives in my hands based on the decisions I made. To say that I faced no repercussions or bias would be disingenuous.

Of all the people I interacted with in the SEAL Teams, about 99% of them were amazing. However, you have that 1% who don't want you to succeed and who'll place roadblocks in your path.

As I started making my way through the process, I was very excited. My OCS package was approved. I was either going to become an officer, or I was going to become a SEAL officer.

Normally, if you have an OCS package, you might be selected to become an officer, but you might not be selected to become a

SEAL officer. And if you're not selected to be a SEAL officer, you have to go into the regular fleet for a couple of years, and then *petition* to become a SEAL officer in order to transition back to the SEAL Teams. And there are very few African American SEALs and even fewer African American SEAL officers.

A Master Chief who I respected and who put me through BUD/S pulled me over to the side and said, "Hey Mark, I understand you're wanting to become an officer. Be careful because it's a different animal that you're facing as an officer."

I was still young and pretty naive. I said, "Oh, Master Chief, come on. It's me. I get along with everybody."

And he looked at me very sternly and said, "Just like I said, be careful because this transition is not going to be what you think. You're going to have a lot of great opportunities, but you're going to have exceptional obstacles to being a successful officer."

That really stuck with me. I'd never thought of that before because the experiences that I had as a minority in a predominately white environment were atypical.

I've been black my whole life. Given the choices that I made— from where I went to college to joining the Navy and joining the SEAL Teams—I knew what I was in for. But it was going to be at another level as an officer.

There were so many small obstacles that people tried to put in my way so I wouldn't succeed.

Putting in an OCS package comes with some very strict guidelines. One of those guidelines is to be interviewed by a panel of officers. Based on that interview, they either recommend you or don't recommend you.

Well, I had my interview and performed well. I made some mistakes because I didn't quite understand the dynamics between officers and enlisted. But the panel was still very impressed, and they gave me an endorsement. Every applicant needed a score of 10 from each of the graders to get approved.

It's important to mention that another black service member was in charge of putting my package together for approval.

I was excited. I was getting my endorsement signatures. Next, I had to go to the officers, have them sign it, and certify it.

One of the officers who interviewed me looked over my package and said, "This isn't right. It has an eight, and I clearly wrote it as a ten."

Turned out that the admin chief had changed my grade from a ten to an eight because he knew that if I didn't get tens across the board, then I wouldn't go on to become an officer.

It's sad because it was done so subtly that had the officer not reviewed it carefully, I would've gotten all the signatures, but wouldn't have become an officer.

That was a huge lesson. It went right back to what the Master Chief had said. I thought that it'd be my white counterparts who didn't want me to succeed. But in this instance, it was another black sailor who didn't want me to succeed.

He purposely sabotaged me. That chief knew how hard the road would be for a black man, and he did it anyway. I was absolutely floored that somebody would go to that effort.

At my new command, I let them know that my officer candidate package was en route and being processed, but I planned on supporting this team for my three-year tour just in case my package was declined.

They all knew that when you apply for OCS you've been in the Teams for a while. It also meant that they realized they'd lose me after a year because I had a very strong chance of making the cut and getting selected as a SEAL Officer candidate.

Jay, the Master Chief in charge of Sniper School, who I was working for, looked at my package and said, "Yeah, okay, we're losing this guy in a couple months."

The process for submitting your package takes months—six to eight months. Add to that, I'd also transitioned from the West Coast to the East Coast.

I talked to an admin officer who happened to be another African American gentleman. I asked him if he mailed my package. And he said, "No, nope. Son, you have plenty of time. I'll make sure to get to it."

I asked every couple of weeks and still *nothing*. The deadline was coming up and one day, he was gone. So I had somebody in admin pull my package and made a copy of the complete package. I mailed it just a couple days before the deadline.

In the meantime, someone told me that the admin officer wasn't very supportive of my transition from enlisted to officer. Surprise, surprise.

My package shipped out. I confirmed that it was received before the deadline. Then, I went back to that admin officer and said, "Hey, sir, the deadline passed. Were you able to mail out my package?"

He very nonchalantly said, "Mark, you know, I totally forgot about that. But well, you're young, you can just resubmit."

I said, "You know, sir, I figured you were going to do that. So I made a copy of my package and shipped it off anyway, and it was received. I just wanted to let you know that I already knew that you weren't going to send that."

He was enraged that I'd gone behind his back, had taken care of my own career, and that by doing those things, I had taken him out of the position where he was the final say on whether or not that package got sent off. He hadn't done his job, and yet he was angry because he knew I was gonna get selected. He simply didn't want it to happen.

When I look back at this experience, I liken it to expecting to get hit by a train. Imagine being told that you have to walk down these train tracks in order to get to your destination. The one caveat is that you're going to get hit if you take your eyes off the prize for even a second.

I know what a train looks like, sounds like, and feels like when it's barreling down the tracks relentlessly and mindlessly heading towards its destination. While walking, I'm constantly looking down the tracks, ready to move out of the way of the train that's supposed to hit me.

I can smell the oil from the thousands of trains that have come down these tracks over the years. Feel the gravel between the railroad ties, hear the birds squawking, and the feeling of boredom as my long rhythmic strides bring me ever closer to the end of my journey.

I'm almost to my destination and I see the train station up ahead and realize that I've made it. All of a sudden, I'm run over by something I didn't expect. I look up and I see something totally out of place on train tracks.

Instead of getting hit by the train that I was expecting, I was instead hit by one of those stupid service vehicles that is equipped to drive down the tracks. At that point, all I can think in my head is the Master Chief looking at me and shaking his head and saying in a way that only a father or mentor can say, *I never said you'd get hit by a train.*

15

A PAINFUL DECISION

I was an Air Force brat, which means my father was in the military, and for most of my young life, we were traveling all around the world, taking in lots of interesting experiences. When I followed in his footsteps and joined the military at twenty-four, my dad was very proud.

And like most father-son relationships, at some point, ours had become strained. Looking back, I know my dad did the best he could.

He was married at eighteen, joined the military, and had his first kid at nineteen. He was still growing up. I mean, eighteen years old is basically still a kid. And going off on your own to join the military ...

Well, all those things were incredible stressors. Add to that having your first kids—two babies before you're twenty-three years old. I can't imagine how challenging that was, can you?

Even with all of that, my dad was always present. He got home at about the same time every day. He was always at football practices.

He was always at football games and basketball games. My dad was really involved.

And he was also very strict but fair. Of course, when you're a kid, you don't understand that strictness is for your benefit.

My dad was the biggest person I've ever known. He was the first man I saw as my mentor, my disciplinarian, my biggest cheerleader, and my therapist. I was lucky in that regard because that's who my father was to me.

I believe a dad should be all of those things. I think because my dad truly was so many things to me, I thought he was indestructible. I'd never seen him cry or meltdown.

Then, one day when he was in his early fifties, Dad was cutting the grass, slipped, pulled a muscle, and went on about his day. No big deal. He visited the doctor.

The doctor told him, "Hey, you're getting to be up in age. You just pulled a muscle. Take some Motrin. You're gonna be fine."

A couple of months went by, and the pains weren't really going away. So he finally went to the hospital. They did some X-rays and sent him home.

He left the hospital, got home, and he already had five messages telling him that he needed to come right back to the hospital. The Air Force Base where we lived was maybe fifteen minutes from the hospital. In a span of fifteen minutes, they had already called him repeatedly. He and my mother knew something bad had happened.

He drove right back to the hospital.

In the X-rays, they'd just seen that he had a mass on his hipbone. So they performed an immediate biopsy and got the results back.

When my dad was fifteen, he fractured his hip. And through that injury, he developed something called chondrosarcoma, which is a very rare bone cancer. It was so rare that I think there were only 1,000 cases per year in the United States at the time.

In my dad's fall, he had actually fractured his hip. Meanwhile, that cancer had been growing very slowly and finally reached the point where it made the hip bone brittle. During the two months that he was just taking Motrin, the cancer was aggressively spreading throughout his body.

It was right around Christmas when we headed back to the doctor. Since the cancer was so aggressive, the doctor scheduled surgery for a hip replacement. If all went according to plan, they'd get all of the cancer, replace his hip and send him home to live the rest of his long life with a big scar and a good story of how he beat cancer.

When my family arrived at the Ohio State University Hospital, the lead surgeon explained the procedure and basically said, "Hey, we're gonna go in there, clear out all the cancer, and then we're going to replace his hip. He'll be fine."

About thirty or forty-five minutes into the surgery, the doctors came back out, which I knew wasn't a good sign. They told me that once they got inside and opened him up, they could see that the cancer had spread to different parts of his body.

His hip had been destroyed to the point where they said, "Hey, look. We're gonna have to take your father's leg."

My mom got the news and was incapable of making a decision. The doctor needed an answer, so I listened to him and got all the information. Then, I just asked him one simple question.

"Will this save my dad's life?"

He told me that it would. So I said, "Go ahead and do what you need to do. You have my permission to amputate his leg."

At that point in my life, it was the absolute hardest conversation because I knew that my dad had gone under anesthesia thinking he would get a new hip. But when he woke up, he was going to come out of surgery with no new hip *and no leg*.

The operation was taking hours, and the time just didn't seem to be moving. It was as if time itself was at a complete standstill. But he finally came out and was in recovery.

I don't know if you've seen movies where there's a scene happening in a normal hallway of a house, probably no more than fifteen feet long, but they stretch it out so that it feels like a mile. As I was walking into my dad's recovery room, that's what I felt like.

I knew what I was about to see would change my life forever. But I also knew that my father's life was just changed in a way that he wouldn't fully come to grips with for quite some time.

It felt as though hours passed on that trip into his room. Walking into the room and seeing him without his leg … He went from the biggest person I'd ever seen to looking like an infant. This man who'd always been a giant in my life has just transformed in front of me.

Even at this moment, I still have no words … I wish I could describe it, but I can't.

He was coming out of the anesthesia. As he was kind of waking up, the first person he saw was me. And he just looked at me, smiled, and said, "Hey, buddy, how are you doing?"

I was absolutely heartbroken.

Once the anesthesia wore off, reality would sink in for my dad. He was about to be hit with the awareness that his leg was gone. And all I could think about was the fact that I was the one who had to make a life-changing decision for my dad.

And as I said, it was a hard decision to make. But to see the results of that decision was haunting. I felt an overwhelming sense of guilt knowing what was coming when he realized that a huge part of his body was gone forever.

Just like before, this was the perfect time to let the grief that I was experiencing take its natural course and just let it all out. The familiar lump was in my throat, my heart was racing again, and the vice grip was back, squeezing my chest even harder than it had when we lost Michael. Still, the tears wouldn't come.

I didn't experience anger this time, only sadness. Not normal sadness, but the sadness that extends to the depths of your soul.

All I could think was, *I have changed his life forever.*

Fast forward. He was having complications and they'd performed multiple surgeries, but he seemed like he was getting better. And he was improving ... until he wasn't.

He wasn't feeling well again.

When the doctors talked to me about the cancer, they told me that if the cancer came back, it would be inoperable. "There's nothing we can do. We're not going to do radiation. We're not going to do chemo because once it comes back, it is vicious and brutal. And it'll go on forever. And it'll just kill him."

Four months later, he still wasn't feeling better. The doctors confirmed it was cancer. Knowing there was no remedy for it, I had to watch my father die over a very short amount of time.

The silver lining is that even though we had experienced a falling out and some rough patches, I got to see my dad every weekend for several months because I was instructing in sniper school, and it was only a two-hour drive from my house.

I would finish up on Saturdays and go hang out with my dad, tell stories, and get to know him better and understand what his life was like. He was so happy because in those last six months, he had changed his perspective. He let me know that he appreciated me as a son and was proud of everything that I had accomplished.

But to me, everything I'd accomplished paled in comparison to what he was going through. Not once did my dad complain. He never expressed feeling sorry for himself. He just took it all on the chin and showed gratitude for every day he had left.

To this day, I am so proud of my dad because of the way he handled adversity, cancer, and unexpected amputation. He just kept going and wouldn't quit. Although it was devastating, it was also beautiful to get to share that time with him. That time was a treasure.

Even though I lost the biggest influence in my life, I had the opportunity to reconcile and get to know my dad and what made him tick. He was an exceptional man and what he instilled in me from a very young age has helped me tremendously throughout my entire life.

I remembered the words that my BUD/S Instructor told me after Hell Week. Everything you've experienced in life, how your parents raised you, and your success and failures have prepared you to be a Navy SEAL.

During those final months with my dad, those words played in my head over and over, and I was watching the biggest influence in my life still making a difference through such adversity. I couldn't have become the man I am today without the man that shaped everything about me throughout my life.

If you're reading this chapter and your father played an active role in your life, please give your father a call, give him a hug, and thank him. If you've had a falling out, reconcile with him because they're only in your life for a short time. Please don't let another day pass without connecting.

16

OFFICER CANDIDATE SCHOOL

A s I approached the end of my Sniper School Instructor Duty in the fall of 2003, I was going home after work every day to play with my kids and enjoy as much time as possible with them. My daughter Rylie was five and my son Braden was one and a half.

That's when I was chosen for Officer Candidate School. It was time to prepare to go from Virginia Beach down to Pensacola, Florida, and transition from being an enlisted man to becoming a Navy SEAL officer. Officer Candidate School lasted three months.

If you don't already know, it's very similar to the movie *An Officer and a Gentleman* in some ways. There's always someone watching your every step, pointing out all of your mistakes, and finding the energy to yell at the top of their lungs well into the evening.

It's a really difficult transition because you separate from the Navy for about twenty-four hours, and the person you were, the accomplishments you achieved, and the life you knew come to a screeching halt and are replaced by a man in a funny hat who has the duty to get you ready for the leadership and responsibilities of a military officer.

The enlisted contract on which you entered the Navy is void, and you reenter the Navy as a naval officer candidate. You also change source rating from an enlisted code to the code of an officer, where you officially become a US Navy officer.

Going into OCS, you know the experience is going to be different. You know you're going to be in a leadership position, and you know that OCS is going to suck. Not in the same ways as BUD/S, but OCS and the United States Marine Corps (USMC) drill instructors are an entity unto themselves and are professionals at making life challenging for anyone who aspires to become an officer.

They take their jobs very seriously and are the most feared individuals in Pensacola, Florida—except if you're a Navy SEAL. With my background, it became a game to see who would win the battle of wills and how to figure out the Love/Hate relationship that is Drill Instructor and Officer Candidate.

Throughout my experience, I grew to appreciate their job and endure the thirteen weeks of reindeer games that slowly turned civilians into very capable and professional naval officers. Everything I got to do as an enlisted SEAL all went away, and I had to focus on this management track.

It was super interesting. Even though I was in the military and knew the systems and how everything worked, the transition of becoming an officer still made me pretty anxious. I didn't know if I was going to be any good at it.

When I checked in, I learned we had a class of eighty-four. It was disorienting because we were all kept up a lot and were just trying to figure out how things worked. We had about three or four days of waiting as they processed us in before we actually started Officer Candidate School.

And they had these dreadful Marine drill instructors. They're exceptional at their jobs. They have to take a program designed to take young men and women (who are only twenty-two or twenty-three years old) off the street and make them into military officers in a relatively short amount of time.

Everything was on a very strict timeline. There were very strict rules. We had objectives we had to meet. But for these eighty-four children who had just become mine, this was all a brand new experience.

Keep in mind, I was thirty-two. That made me nine years older than most of the class. To see the faces of these young people— they had just been in college, partying and being college students, and suddenly, they were in the military, not just playing video games. This was real.

The second I saw my class, I knew I had to take a leadership position and make sure that these young people survived their indoctrination into the Navy. They didn't just seem like babies—they *looked* like babies. They hadn't really experienced much in life yet.

Having completed my career as an enlisted SEAL and my service as an instructor at Sniper School, I knew this school was gonna be a pain in the butt and stupid and just one of those things you had to endure. These students were in for the biggest transition of their lives.

I quickly learned that I had to take these eighty-four kids and act as their parent, their disciplinarian, their planner, their psychologist, and their mentor. And I had to embody what a SEAL was supposed to be and what a leader was supposed to be.

But strangely, I didn't know if I'd be any good at it.

We had transitioned from getting all the administrative stuff done in the first couple of days. Officer Candidate School really began when the drill instructors arrived. It was like a tornado ... bodies were flying around, beds were getting flipped over, and there was so much yelling.

It was total chaos.

And as I watched it, I momentarily got swept up in it, but then I took a step back and saw it for what it was. Some of those kids had never been yelled at before. They'd never been up at four in the morning.

They were completely unprepared for what was about to happen. It dawned on me that I'd have to lead each of them individually to make sure that the entire class survived.

I wasn't doing great academically, but I didn't care because it didn't really prove anything. I was spending ninety percent of my time managing the class to make sure that they were doing well.

Physically, I was slightly out of shape, but it wasn't a big deal. However, I had to do what's called "leading from the front." That meant I did everything first, so I was trying to be the fastest in the class.

I had to be in their corner and be a cheerleader, but also remain stoic and separated at the same time because I couldn't play favorites. I had to represent our class well and stand up for them.

I had to take the brunt of what the drill instructors and staff were dishing out to us. I had to take it and manage it so my class didn't have to worry about it, and they could just concentrate on being students and get through the process.

We had an inspection that we did an exceptional job on. Because of it, they got to see and appreciate what *I* had to go through. In turn, I appreciated what *they* had to go through because I was watching them grow.

They were relying on me to guide them. It was fun to watch the lights come on. And it was fun to go through the process of watching them grow, watching them stumble, and *become*. Slowly, I watched them gain their own wings and learn to fly on their own.

Over the course of the three months, I was coming to love all my classmates.

I didn't like them all, but they were mine. They were my problem children. And I defended them because I was responsible for all eighty-four of them.

I learned that leadership has much less to do with leading and much more about playing all the other vital roles. I couldn't get a lot of the stuff finished that I needed because the students were always coming to me with their problems.

One of the officers pulled me aside and told me I was doing a great job, but I disagreed with him. I said, "Sir, I can't get anything done because I'm doing all these other things. I'm not able to lead."

He said, "That's what leadership is. You can tell you're a good leader because these students still come to you with their problems. Once the people you're leading stop coming to you with their problems, then you're failing as a leader.

"And you said you can't keep your head above water and excel the way you want to because you're doing the leadership role as the class leader, and that's to be expected. You're not going to do great in some aspects, but you're gonna excel in others."

I took that as an important lesson learned.

I was able to take that leadership role without having led a team before. Even though the SEAL Teams are small, they're very structured. As a junior SEAL, you don't lead anybody—*you* are your own leader. You have a chief, another junior officer, a leading petty officer, and the people who have experience over you. So you're really learning about leading.

Decades later, I'm still in contact with some of those students. I developed such rewarding relationships because of the experience that I had as a leader of my class. I have since been able to take what I've learned in that short three months and apply it to leading SEALs. Not only would I use it for leading SEALs in general, but also for leading SEALs in combat over several combat deployments.

I would recommend that everyone take a leadership role in the military or in a university. Anywhere you have a chance to lead, mentor, solve problems, or work in very dynamic situations is key because those are skills you're going to need throughout life.

17

SWIMMING ANTICS

One of the funniest things that happened at Officer Candidate School was a day at the pool.

Normally, our days are pretty packed, down to the minute. But we had a day where the drill instructors weren't around, and we were going to do water survival and swimming stuff all day.

Now, keep in mind, there was (and is) a stigma that a lot of African Americans aren't good swimmers. And I was always aware of that stigma existing at boot camp—even at BUD/S or SEAL selection, the instructor staff were always overly cautious of my ability and other black students' ability to swim.

I knew this going into our pool day. As a class, we were all getting changed out on the pool deck. There was a guy giving the safety briefing to all of us before the evolutions for the day at the pool. But he was looking directly at me when he talked about water safety, being safe in the water, and how close you could get to people.

I was well aware of what was happening. I knew that in his mind he was thinking, *I have to watch this guy because he's black, and he's not going to be able to swim like the rest of them. I have to keep in serious contact with this guy.*

He made himself my shadow for the duration of the day. When we were starting to do things, I intentionally acted like I was struggling in the water. And I told a couple of the other students I was with, "Hey, just act like you're helping me a lot and be concerned for my safety."

Everybody was in on the joke.

We were going through the exercises, and we were all playing our part. I swam up and down the pool, and my new shadow was literally walking down the pool deck right beside me the entire time. After a couple of hours, I was getting tired of dealing with him.

A couple of the other students were diving down to the bottom of the pool, and I did the same thing. I dove to the bottom of the pool, and I looked up to see this guy's silhouette jumping up and down. So I swam to the surface.

He was freaking out, "Sir, sir, sir, you can't do that. You can't go underwater and stay down there."

I said, "Well, the other students are doing that. Why can't I do it?"

The look on his face told me he wanted to say, "Because you're black and you can't swim!" He was prepared to jump in the water to save my life. He'd made me his sole focus and only mission.

I'm sure during the safety brief, he was taking inventory. *Okay, there's a black guy, a couple black students …* But I'd had enough. I was finally done with him.

As I got to the surface, the look on my face rather pointedly questioned him. *Why are you looking at me?* I knew he so badly wanted to answer, "Because you can't swim and I need to protect you from yourself."

I went under the water again, and the same thing happened. But there were *two* instructors watching me this time. Now, they were both coming over to me in a ridiculous panic, saying, "You can't keep doing what you're doing because you know—" And they both stopped themselves before they said what they were really thinking.

Truth be told, I was actually showing off a little because our pool time was almost up. About that time, my drill instructor sneaked into class. I saw him observing and realized that he could see exactly what was happening.

Finally, he looked across the pool and yelled, "He's a Navy SEAL, you idiots!"

I'll never forget the look on their faces. They couldn't begin to hide their embarrassment, shock, and utter disbelief. But we weren't quite finished. I had a bit more fun yet to play on my shadow.

The final thing we had to do was a relay race. So I started the swim and I out-swam everybody by a lot. I just kind of looked at them as I got out of the pool, smiled, and said, "I bet you didn't expect that. The guy that you were so worried about was actually an expert swimmer and one of the best swimmers and divers in the world."

I always get this small sense of glee when I break people's perception of me and make them look at themselves and think, *I got that one wrong.*

18

BIKE-RIDING LESSON

A Navy SEAL buddy of mine, Rich Diviney, often tells the story of someone asking his son how cool it was that his dad was a Navy SEAL. His kid said he wished his dad was the garbage truck man. A couple more questions revealed that all his son truly wanted was for his dad to be home more often.

Even though certain professions carry an air of mystery or prestige, that doesn't make up for responsibilities that come with being a parent. One of my greatest joys in life is being a dad. I can't even begin to tell you how happy it makes me.

Rylie was born in 1998, not long before my first deployment, and Braden came along four years later in 2002, right before we left San Diego.

My son Braden has always been a treasure. He and I were inseparable for all his young life. Where I went, there he was. A constant companion that I relied upon more than I realized.

We were growing up together, he as a child and I as a young Navy SEAL, trying to figure life out. But as long as we were hanging out, life was ok.

When I wasn't his on-call jungle gym, I was his giant teddy bear that always got so much joy in hearing his infectious laughter, or looking the other way when he did something he wasn't supposed to do—so much delight from my pint-sized little man.

One day stands out more than others. The day I taught my son how to ride a bike. A bike was not only a two-wheeled machine, but it was a two-wheeled ticket to freedom. A way to explore his world as fast as those tiny legs would take him (usually not farther than three blocks), but to a four-year-old, three blocks was as great a distance as 300 miles.

One day, he was frustrated by his training wheels, and I knew he was ready to take the leap of riding his freedom machine on his own. I did what any good father would do. I took off the training wheels and told him that yesterday was the last day with them.

There was the tiniest decline on the sidewalk in front of the house. The sun was bright, the wind was in our faces, and I knew this was the day to let my son take the reins of his own freedom.

He was in his normal uniform of mismatched shoes, no socks, shorts that were a little too big, and a Star Wars shirt.

He looked at his bike without the training wheels and for a second, there was a look of panic because he knew he was getting ready to embark on his first taste of freedom. There was also a look of anger as if he was saying, "How can you do this to me today of all days?"

But we put his helmet on, and I explained to him that as long as he trusts me, he'll never need those stupid training wheels again. I told him to keep pedaling and I would take care of everything else.

I put my hand on the bike seat and he looked back to make sure my hand didn't leave that damn seat because he wasn't sure what riding without his training wheels would feel like, but he did know what falling off a bike felt like.

The first time I kept my hand on the seat and told him to not stop pedaling, no matter what. We did that for about ten minutes. Each time, I took a little more pressure off the seat and let him figure out his balance as he was pedaling on his own.

The final step was to hold the seat while walking next to him. He saw me next to him, and in a flash, looked back at the seat to make sure my hand was still where it was supposed to be. It was, but barely.

We did that a few more times and my final step was to walk beside him, but with no pressure on the seat. Unbeknownst to him, he was riding all on his own and he was hauling ass with those little legs moving as fast as he could. He didn't even realize that I was running next to him.

It took him a few seconds for his brain to register that I was running beside him and not holding his seat. He squealed with absolute delight and screamed out, "I dood it, Daddy! I dood it all by myself!"

I can't express the joy I felt at that moment. My wonderful, beautiful son had dood it all by himself!

19

THE TOOTHBRUSHING SONG

The same year that Braden learned how to ride a bike, Evan Elise was born. Evan has always been special. She's so incredibly smart that it's unnerving sometimes.

All my kids are brilliant. My daughter Rylie and my daughter Olivia (who made a surprise appearance later) are both brilliant. My son Braden is equally brilliant. In fact, when we lived in Germany, we had to attend a parent teacher conference where we were informed that our son was one of the smartest students that they've ever taught.

We were beaming with pride and confirmed that we agreed with their assessment of our son. His praise was immediately followed by, "He's the smartest we've seen in a while, but he's also the laziest." Pride faded into a nod of confirmation from his parents because he was amazingly lazy when he's bored.

But Evan was on another level.

She was also a daddy's girl, and we share a love for music. When she was three years old and refused to brush her teeth, I made up a song on the spot so she would be motivated to do it anyway.

E-E-E is for Evan Elise, Evan Elise, Evan Elise. E-E-E is for Evan Elise and you know she is so so sweet. So so sweet, So so sweet, the prettiest girl that you ever would meet. So so sweet, so so sweet, the sweetest little thing that you ever would meet—SPIT.

Of course, I had to add "spit" because she was only three and needed a signal that now is the time to spit out the toothpaste. We'd repeat that song until the ritual was done. (Best song ever by the way.)

She always had a knack for music, and even though I have an awful singing voice, that was our thing.

One day, we were making the ten-hour drive home for Christmas, and we had the music blaring, as was our ritual, and I noticed that she was singing every song on the radio.

I asked her how she knew all of these songs. Without skipping a beat, she says, "I remember everything I hear," and continues to sing the song perfectly. Not only did she sing it perfectly, she continued on for another few hours until she fell asleep.

However, when we took her to preschool, she never spoke to her teachers. We were called into a parent/teacher conference where her teachers were concerned because they didn't know if Evan was falling behind or just couldn't speak.

With a huge sigh, the teacher explained that, "We can't assess Evan, because she hasn't said a word all year." That was so strange because that girl spoke constantly around her family. Almost nonstop.

She had a talent for taking in vast amounts of information and was fully aware of everything around her. She had a knack for reading body language and understanding adults and adult humor.

One day, a few years later, her second-grade teacher was talking to the class and said a very adult joke under her breath. The joke went over all the children's heads—all except one child. From the back of the room, there was this very light chuckle that was followed by, "That was really funny."

Her understanding of adults and adult situations is key because when I was struggling later to perform a simple task in Home Depot, Evan knew that something wasn't right with her dad. More on that later.

20

THE FOURTH AND FINAL TIME

One of my most difficult transitions was the transition from being operational—deploying during wartime multiple times—to becoming a student at grad school. That transition came with a lot of insecurity because I, as you remember, flunked out of college and was adrift.

Even though I completed my bachelor's, that experience was still dragging me down. When I knew I needed a break, I contacted the SEAL Detailer (the person who gives you all of your career placement), and she let me know the programs that were available.

I was just planning on going and sitting around for two years, reading a lot of books and taking a break while getting an education. However, our detailer was very smart. She'd been in her position for a long, long time.

She said, "It's time to get your MBA because you have so many damn kids that you're going to need a good job when you're too old to shoot guns and run around the desert."

The level of fear that I had was practically palpable, so I said, "No, no, no, I can't go get my MBA. I'm not good at math, I flunked out of college. And, you know, this is not going to be the right career progression for me."

I showed up at Naval Postgraduate School, having done mediocre-at-best in my previous college career. I was going to learn business at the graduate level … and I was absolutely terrified.

I started the course. It was a firehose on full blast. I was starting from zero and really struggling, but I kept my head above water. She was right, I had the ability to do it. I just had to work extremely hard.

For the first part of it, the garbage in, garbage out, I wasn't good at that (and still struggle, even to this day). I couldn't figure out what was important to know. For me, everything seemed important.

I'd never been talented at understanding the material and knowing when something was important enough to be tested on. However, for the analytics part—which was the second part of grad school where we took case studies, dissected them, and developed critically thought-out answers—I did exceptionally well.

The first thing I heard at The Naval Postgraduate School orientation for grad school is, "You're going to leave here with one of the three D's: a diploma, a divorce, or a dependent." I left with two of the three.

I eventually earned my Master's of Business Administration with a focus on Financial Management. The curriculum was demanding, the hours were long, but the pace was a welcome break from the combat deployments that had become the norm for Clan Greene.

When I embraced the break that was originally supposed to be time to relax and reconnect with my family, I found myself working unbelievably hard just to keep up.

There I was, learning business at the graduate level. A daunting task no matter your background, but even more for me since I had graduated with a degree in Criminology (not math-intensive since I absolutely suck at math).

However, getting my MBA was the goal, and I attacked that goal like I attacked every other challenge I faced in the Navy. The semesters passed, and I was finally getting the hang of school.

My diploma was within reach. I was not getting a divorce (yet), but something was wrong. My wife's cycle was late. She was only late when she was pregnant, but that was impossible because we didn't plan on having any more children. Three was more than enough because we were officially outnumbered and barely keeping our parental heads above water.

One week late stretched into two, and we both knew what happened. She was indeed pregnant with baby number four. *Shit!!! We can't do this now. I'm in my final stretch of school.*

When I looked at the calendar, I realized baby number four was due right about the time I would be working on my graduate thesis. *Shit. Shit. Shit.*

What was I going to do with a fourth kid? I love my kids, but the thought of number four felt like it was going to be the straw that broke the camel's back. Before I knew it, my wife was in labor again, and I was minutes away from sleepless nights, the grind of a thesis and three relentless kids that didn't care about the outside world.

When Olivia (Livi) came, she was ugly just like the rest of them at birth, but there was something different about her. Instead of panic, there was a lot of excitement. All of her siblings thought that she was "their baby" and really helped out much more than kids their age should have been able to help.

But the other thing that changed is that she absolutely adored me. There wasn't the break-in period where I couldn't be around because I didn't have anything she needed.

Olivia needed her daddy from day one. I'm 6'2" and 225 pounds with unusually huge hands. Huge like catcher's mitt huge, and my brand new 6-pound baby fit perfectly. Her head, shoulder, and belly fit in the palm of my hands. And her adorable little legs draped over my forearm like two perfectly sized frog legs.

She was with me at all times … when I was vacuuming the carpet, walking the dog, cooking dinner, or watching TV with the rest of Clan Greene.

When she was hungry, she wanted her dad. When she needed a nap, she wanted her dad. When she woke up in the middle of the night, she wanted her dad.

I didn't put that kid down until she was about six months old. Her head still fit in the palm of my hand, but the rest of her was strategically placed in a way that her tiny little legs fit perfectly against my stomach.

Baby number four was an enormous blessing like all the rest, and Livi still needs her dad when she's crying, when she's hungry, or when she's having a hard day.

Some of my fondest memories are being able to hold both baby Livi and little Evan at the same time. I always seemed to have a kid draped over a forearm or somewhere on or around me. It was a relief to know my schedule for an uninterrupted year and a half. However, over the horizon, I was getting back to the business of preparing for combat operations all over the world, with a schedule that did not include my kids, tickle time, being a human jungle gym, or anything that resembled a normal day in the life of a father of four.

I was preparing for the unpredictable, and when I made it back to my SEAL Team, my predictions were more than I could even anticipate.

21

AN UNLIKELY PAIRING

A s I was approaching the end of grad school, I called the detailer and let her know that I wanted to go back to my SEAL Teammates and be the Officer in Charge.

She pulled some strings, and I got my assignment. I was walking through school and ran into the new batch of officers that were coming through grad school. A gentleman named Bobby walked up, we greeted each other, and he said, "Hey, where are you going for your Officer in Charge tour?"

"Oh, I'm going to SEAL Team EIGHT," I said.

One of the first things that the officer asked was, "Who's your chief?" because that relationship is exceptionally important. So I told Bobby that they told me the guy's name was Rob.

His expression changed. He said, "No, no, I don't think you understand. Like, who's your chief gonna be?"

I repeat, "The name's Rob 'X.'"

Bobby looked at me in disbelief and said, "You need to talk to XO when you get to your command because, I don't know if you know this, the guy who's gonna be your chief used to be a skinhead when he was younger."

As you probably know, it's an understatement to say that African Americans and skinheads don't mix all that well. So I wasn't prepared for what was coming next.

I was getting ready to go pick up my own platoon, and you only have one shot to get this tour right, being a fairly new officer. I was coming into a SEAL platoon after being away from the SEAL community. I'd finished a tour at the boat team, and then I had about two years of grad school. So I'd been out of the SEAL platoon for almost four years.

All of a sudden, I was going back into it *at what I thought* was a huge, huge disadvantage. I got ready to transition back to Virginia from California. And I made a conscious decision that I'd solidified in Officer Candidate School—everybody deserves a clean slate.

Providing everyone with a clean slate is the only way I know how to interact with people, and my chief was going to receive the same treatment as everyone else. His past had nothing to do with me, and I had to assume that what he did in the past would not affect our relations as platoon leadership.

We had a job to do and a combat deployment to prepare for. I made up my mind at that moment that no matter what my platoon chief's past might be, I wouldn't let that affect how we'd lead and how we'd act as a platoon. Rob turned out to be the absolute best chief I'd ever had. He and I got along exceptionally well.

One day, several months into our workup cycle, we were finished with the training block and I knew something was bothering Rob. We had been working together closely for six or seven months, and I had a feeling I already knew what was weighing on him.

Rob asked if we could talk. In this talk, Rob starts telling me, "When you're younger, you make some decisions that aren't really who you are ... You meet people who just really change your perspective ... Who you are as a kid isn't who you are as an adult ...

"I have something I need to tell you," he said.

I casually responded, "You mean when you were a skinhead as a kid?"

Rob's jaw dropped. "You knew this whole time?! How did you find out?!"

"I met someone who worked with you and he said, 'Bro, do you know who Rob is? He has some sketchy tattoos ...'"

"I've had those covered up! Why didn't you say something?" Rob asked.

"Rob, I don't care. You and I have to work together to make sure this platoon is a good one. We need to be able to work well together in combat. We have a great relationship and I consider you a good friend. Everybody deserves a clean slate," I said.

After that, our relationship improved even more. He introduced me to his family. We even had a nickname for our duo: Big and Rob. There was a show on MTV about the life and times of an unlikely friendship that shouldn't have stood the test of time, let alone flourish.

The guy called Big was this mountain of a black man, standing well over six feet. On the flip side, Rob was much more height-challenged. So, the contrast between them was the obvious thing that immediately stood out to most. You had to pay attention to see that they were best friends and always had each other's backs, usually in very comical ways.

The platoon gave us the nickname Big and Rob because we always had each other's backs and were inseparable when it came to decision-making and leading. We didn't always agree and oftentimes argued behind closed doors about a decision that needed to be made. But when we presented the decision to the platoon, it wasn't up for discussion—the decision was final.

We *always* supported each other in public. That was all that mattered.

The lessons I learned from OCS and, more importantly, the lessons I learned from my experienced platoon and my challenging platoon helped solidify my leadership style and how I was going to lead alongside my new chief.

My chief's background ended up being the least of my worries when I showed up at SEAL Team EIGHT and met my platoon for the first time.

22

MEETING MY PLATOON

Getting your SEAL platoon is the pinnacle of your time as a SEAL officer. You only get this one chance to shine, to lead the most highly skilled and qualified warriors for four years in the US military. And with that comes a lot of challenges because most of the guys are absolutely brilliant.

They think outside the box, they challenge you, and they can be downright hard to lead because they know what strong leadership and poor leadership look like. Each day is a test to make sure you're the right type of leader.

This testing phase is relentless, and it comes from every member of the platoon. Sometimes they're just not going to follow you. They can make or break your experience.

I was determined to make an incredibly good group and create a remarkable experience. But as I said earlier, I'd already started off on a potential negative because of my chief's history.

The Executive Officer was an exceptional operator and leader who I'd known throughout my entire career. He was on his way to reach the pinnacle of SEAL leadership in the Naval Special Warfare community. The mere mention of his name garnered respect at all levels of Naval Special Warfare.

When I showed up, I met him and was happy to see him. As we talked, he explained to me that we needed to expand by two platoons. When they do an expansion like that, they have to pick from the existing platoons and make a new platoon out of the remaining operators.

I got my platoon and asked around about them. A lot of the SEALs were not wanted by the other platoons. I went back to the XO and said, "Hey, I was asking around, and my platoon is made up of the problem children from the team."

That XO looked me dead in the eye and said, "Mark, you're an older and more experienced operator, and you have I have history. I'm not going to put you in a position where you won't succeed. I gave you this team because they're great guy and they're very talented. They definitely come with leadership challenges, but I know that you're going to do a great job with them."

I took a deep breath, looked him in the eye, shook his hand, and said, "Okay," because I trusted him.

My XO was a standout leader in the SEAL community and a phenomenal SEAL in every way. However, I didn't tell him about the dynamic with my new chief because he would've had a fit and changed some things up.

I got to my platoon, and I met them for the first time. They were cocky and arrogant and really good at their jobs, but they were fairly young. And I immediately loved all of them. Learning their history was going to be a priority.

I just sat back and observed them for a couple of months. We got on our first trips, but I didn't say a whole lot. I was just observing. I wanted to figure out who the leader of this hodgepodge group of guys was. I figured it out pretty early on, but there were some subtleties that had to play out.

Once I knew who the ringleader was, I then determined the pecking order of my experienced guys and my new guys. At the same time, I was also trying to gauge the relationship I'd have with my chief.

I had a lot of things going on, and I felt a little overwhelmed. But I knew it was going to be okay because I genuinely liked the men I was working with.

Fast forward about four months, and I realized the goldmine of talent that I had been gifted. As I began leading, the first thing I told them was, "Look, you guys are experienced. You are in the positions you're in because of your expertise. I trust you, and I'm going to stay out of your way."

Luckily, the platoon leaders merely needed to be given guidelines and simply allowed to go create and do what they do best without me interfering very much. Before I made a decision, I went to the department heads and asked them what they thought. I took all the information and then made a decision.

That one act was something they weren't used to because a lot of leadership in high-performing groups like this tells you what you're going to do and you do it without question. However, I knew that my marauders wouldn't work well that way.

I decided to choose a different approach.

I gave them a say in the direction of the platoon because it was their platoon with sixteen enlisted SEALs and three officers. It was *their* platoon. So I let them run it with one caveat: if you're not running it the right way and I have to stop what I'm doing to go run it for you, then this is *not* going to be a good relationship.

But we all figured it out.

I started to understand the nuances of each individual. One of them stood out because his true passion was to go to Georgia Tech and study brain-actuated prosthesis. Another standout was accepted into Harvard Law School.

Most of them already had degrees, so I wasn't the smartest guy in the room. But I'd earned their respect. The day you know you've earned their respect is when they stop calling you "sir." It's counter-intuitive. If they call you "sir," then they have lower respect for you.

We were on a training trip, and they started calling me by my nickname. Initially, they were making fun of me because I'd made a mistake. (If you made a mistake on the team, they'd capitalize on it.) But I didn't let it bother me, so I was just like, *Okay, that's my nickname.*

In the beginning, they were assholes about it. But after a while I thought, *Fine, that's a great nickname.* So for a year and a half after I got my nickname, I never heard my first name again. I was just that nickname. It was a real show of trust and a high level of loyalty and respect.

One of the other things that I was learning was that they always came to me with their problems. This was good because, *if the people you lead don't come to you with their problems, then you are no longer a good leader.*

They always knew I would take care of them. I stayed consistent, and I let them do what they did best without being required to get information from the Executive Officer (XO), the Commanding Officer (CO), or the Command Master Chief (CMC). They just got to go and excel at what they did best.

They were the best platoon that I'd ever had, but that's just the beginning of the story.

When I got that platoon of sixteen guys, it was hit or miss. It was a true leadership challenge.

One thing that stood out to me from my introduction to the SEAL Teams back in 1993 was how they talked about the dynamics of the team. Even though it was the SEAL *Team*, and we didn't do anything by ourselves, the instructor told us *it's an individual effort to make the team work.*

I had always kept that idea in the back of my mind.

I observed my first platoon and second platoon in my OCS class and had my experience with the boat team. And I incorporated all of that knowledge and experience into my approach.

When I had my eighty-four kids at OCS, I led eighty-four different people in eighty-four different ways to make sure that our team worked. Even when I had my boat team—a small group of eight—it was the same concept.

When I got my platoon teammates, even though the guys could be challenging and headstrong, they were brilliant, vocal, and talented. I had to take the time to see how to lead all sixteen of them individually to make sure that the platoon worked well.

I started with my chief. When Rob and I finally established things, I had to ensure that the dynamic was a strong relationship between us. The way I did this was to discuss with him in detail any decisions that needed to be made before presenting them to the team.

We weren't always going to agree. Sometimes it could get heated, but we would eventually come to an agreement. And once I put that out to the team, that was how we were going to do business.

Now that being said, I presented the way we were going to do things, but oftentimes, Rob also came up with how we were going to do it. We'd go back and forth, and I eventually agreed because he had the most tactical experience. That was how we ran it. And it was a really good dynamic.

That was my first individual on the team. Then, I began leading the ringleader and a couple of others who made sure to not make things easy on me or Rob. This meant that I had to put them in their comfort zone, figure out how they worked best individually, and then let them go do their best work.

The dynamics required that I get buy-in from the older operators because they heavily influenced the younger ones. But I was also involving the newest operators in the decision-making process. They didn't have a filter, so I went up and asked them what they thought about some things. They would tell me, and they usually had exceptional ideas.

They were new to the community, so they processed ideas and solved problems in different ways. Getting that input from them was invaluable. But what I didn't realize was that I was building a strong rapport with everyone at the same time.

The way our team worked, the new guys couldn't be vocal among the old guys, but they could be very vocal with me one-on-one or when I talked to them as a group. The knowledge that they had the autonomy to work on their own built a lot of unit cohesion.

Rob and I dictated which direction the entire team and platoon would go. And I wanted to manage through what I called "course corrections." I wasn't a bully. I wasn't like a bull in a china shop saying, "This is what we're going to do."

It was more like, "Okay, here's what we're going to do. Each of you go out and meet these goals individually so we can make this team work collectively."

Although we initially started off as a hodgepodge of a team, we communicated unusually well. We had an exceptional amount of trust in each other from the top down. We did a lot of things together outside of work, and that translated into all of our scenarios. Even on the battlefield, we were particularly proficient on target.

I genuinely loved my platoon. I didn't like them all. Some of them were just pains in my ass, but they were *my* pains in the ass, and there was a genuine love for each of them.

If I saw any of them on the street today, I'd give them a big hug and thank them for helping me with my transition from graduate school and then to an OIC position because even though I was really good, I was still new to leadership.

I couldn't have done as well as I did without the phenomenal team that I had. I will always have love for that group of sixteen operators because they were extraordinary men, and I'm so very proud of all of them.

23

VISIBLE TRAUMA

In 2015, I was at my final command. I had my final set of orders, and I knew that I was going to retire in 2016. By that time, I would have spent twenty years in SEAL Teams.

There was a sizeable amount of growth, a remarkable number of experiences, and an especially high number of injuries—both visible and invisible. The realization hit that I was going to be doing something else *soon*. And a year to transition was not a lot of time, considering everything I had to get done.

I needed multiple surgeries. There were some things going on with me cognitively that I couldn't articulate because there wasn't a lot of science at the time about trauma.

Back then, we didn't know as much about head injuries. A lot of the things that happen in combat affect you mentally, often resulting in what we now call post-traumatic stress disorder or PTSD.

Not only was I dealing with the aftermath of my military service, but I was also in a scramble to figure out what I was going to do and where I was going to live after I retired.

Most of us—especially if we'd been in for five, ten, fifteen, or twenty years—actually had no idea what was next because we were utterly unprepared for life outside the teams. And the longer we'd been in, the harder the transition would be.

My next stop was the Naval Medical Center up in Bethesda (now the Walter Reed National Military Medical Center) to the National Intrepid Center of Excellence called NICoE and stayed there for a month as an outpatient, getting a head-to-toe examination of everything that was going on with me. I saw psychologists and psychiatrists, did art therapy, practiced a lot of mindfulness exercises, and began to find out exactly what was going on with my brain and body.

With my meticulous nature as an operator, I get more comfort out of knowing exactly what's going on with me—physically and mentally. And sometimes (*a lot of times*) when operators go to NICoE, we actually find out some of the traumatic brain injuries we have and why we're having some cognitive issues.

It's a humbling experience. And it's heartbreaking at some points because you see through the CAT scans and X-rays what's been going on with you and how traumatized you are. There are obviously different levels of trauma, but to see it in a tangible way after experiencing the decline that you've suffered over the course of your career can be tough.

After that month, you invite your spouse and your family up, and the medical staff shares the information. They say, "Here's what's going on with your spouse … your parent …"

Usually, that's what helps. It's a kind of fill-in-the-blanks moment. Then, they discuss how the career, operational tempo, and the injuries could affect your well-being and your quality of life.

That is enlightening, and it gives you a starting point. Right?

Now, you're armed with this knowledge, but you're on the clock because you're not going to have the support that you need to fully take care of yourself in the short amount of time that you have.

You're scrambling because you have this wealth of knowledge, but you don't have a wealth of opportunity and resources to get the specialized help that you need to get better.

In my case, I was coming up on less than a year remaining ...

I'd had a couple of shoulder surgeries, and I got through a lot of the physical ailments. But to touch the things that were happening cognitively? I didn't have enough time.

I just had to continue on with life.

I had to figure out where I was going to work and live. And I had to start going through the transition process, which was so much harder than anything I'd ever endured.

I have no words to describe just how hard that transition process was. I suffered my way through it. My feelings were like a constantly churning wheel ...

I was angry that my family wasn't with me.

I was anxious because I went from being an elite expert to a novice with no goal to focus on.

I was in this vicious cycle of anger, fear, guilt, shame, and sadness.

My identity revolved solely around my life as a SEAL. But I discovered that the very thing my identity came from did not care about me. It didn't have feelings. It couldn't encourage me through leaving the bubble.

I had participated in a couple of transition programs, most notably, with the Honor Foundation, and it started to help. One of the many great things about the Honor Foundation was how it specialized on as many facets of transition as they could cover per cohort, from the perspective of the Special Operations community.

From its inception, the focus of the Honor Foundation has been to help transitioning SEALs, Special Warfare Combat Crewman (SWCCs), and their families. They are masters at exposing us to what transition will look like—in ways that are unique to Special Operations—and equipping us with the tools and framework on how to navigate it.

I was beginning to see my value outside of the military. But I was also beginning to understand that in the SEAL Teams, everybody was special so nobody was special, and I didn't really know what I was good at.

The Honor Foundation did a remarkable job of connecting me with people and programs to show me how my military experience transition translated to the outside world, giving me a boost of much-needed confidence.

I still didn't know what I wanted to do. I was considering taking the easy route and applying for the FBI. I knew the system was still government, and I could join the FBI, take my time, and figure out if it was truly what I wanted to do.

But at the end of the day, I still had to take care of and provide for my family and put them in the best position possible after retirement so their quality of life didn't change. Because I wasn't transitioning alone. *Everybody* was in transition.

I had a daughter who was graduating from high school and moving off to college. My son was going from junior high to high school. There were a lot of moving parts, and it was my sole focus to make each change as seamless as possible.

In doing that, I disregarded myself. And I experienced more suffering through the process.

Hopelessness was waiting there, whispering into the cracks in my mind, threatening my attempts to move forward.

24

LEAVING THE BUBBLE

The most impactful aspect of attending NICoE other than the medical portion was the connections that were made with other operators that were experiencing the ending of their careers the same way I was experiencing mine. Each of us attended the same classes, medical modalities, and shock that we were actually coming to the end of our careers.

My most memorable day was during the final week of the NICoE experience. During our breathing session, we were greeted by something that every special operator dreads ...

A break in our routine.

We had a guest instructor. *Who was this person? Why was she here? I don't know her and I certainly don't trust her.* As we walked in, each of us experienced the intrusion the same way. We assessed the situation to see if it was dangerous. We sized up our opponent. And we determined that she was not welcome.

Just as we were ready to walk out of the class, our regular instructor came in and we all gave a collective sigh of relief. The glares were quickly replaced with smiles and a knowing look to the instructor letting her know that she's not to surprise us again, and this is the last time this is to happen.

Our instructor had grown to enjoy our classes, and in her silent response of a slightly raised eyebrow, the tiniest of smiles, and an almost imperceptible nod, she let us know that she understood, and it won't happen again.

We had a routine of greeting each other with a hug, giving the last guy to show up shit for being late, followed by very juvenile but necessary exchanges of the happenings of the previous night, followed by several bad jokes before we settled into our breathing class.

Our routine was the same for the past three weeks, and our instructor often observed us as we joyfully went through our routine and knew when to jump in and when to let us get through our greeting ritual.

When the guest instructor came in, she wanted to establish herself and her dominance/expertise before we finished our reunion ritual. This was a huge mistake.

The more she tried to intervene, the more she was ignored until very quietly, our normal instructor touched her arm and said, "Just watch. They do this every morning and it's really fascinating because even though they seem like they haven't seen each other for weeks, they actually just saw each other last night during dinner. They'll let us start when they're done, but I highly suggest you not interrupt how they start their day. I've really grown to love how they so eagerly connect each morning."

As a group, we all knew that we were about to leave our protective environment and get thrown back into reality in just a few days. We had a wealth of information, a new sense of accomplishment, and tools that could help us integrate into our daily routine, and officially start the retirement process. I left that Friday confident, but realistic in the fact that once I walked out that front door, I was on my own and still not completely ready to face retirement.

For me, it meant I could actually start the grieving process.

And that's when I went into my first panic ... *This is happening. I'm getting out of the military. There's nothing I can do to stop it.* At this point, everything started to fall apart. I began to realize how unprepared I was for the biggest transition in my life.

There was a fundraiser in New York City, and I was waffling back and forth about going. I didn't really want to be there because I was in kind of a depression. But at the last minute, I decided to go.

I walked up to the venue, and I was the first one there. A gentleman I was talking to for a few minutes said, "Man, you have such an interesting story. Why don't you meet Bill and Kent?"

And I said, "Okay, yeah."

When I met Bill, we hit it off immediately. From the moment we started talking, it seemed like he and I knew each other for many years instead of just a few minutes. He was the most wonderful guy, and he was so proud of me after barely knowing me.

"So you know, you were an enlisted SEAL, you became an officer, and you got your MBA," he said. Then, he added very excitedly, "What's next for you?"

And I looked him straight in the eye and said, "I have absolutely no idea."

Bill's shock was all over his face, and he said, "What do you mean you have no idea?"

I was like, "Bill, I don't know what I'm good at. I've been doing this for so long that I'm really just clueless about what's next."

Kent looked at me in complete bewilderment and asked, "How do you feel about it?"

With zero hesitation, I said, "Bill, Kent, I'm absolutely terrified."

That's when Bill said, "No, no … We can't allow you to be afraid of this process. And what I'm going to do is give you my business card because Kent and I have another engagement to attend. I want you to come out to Los Angeles, and myself, Kent, and my staff—we're going to make sure that you're taken care of."

I had no idea what to do or what to say. But my first inclination was, *Why?*

"Why would you—as a stranger—after talking to me for two hours, offer for me to come out to Los Angeles, pay for everything, and meet your staff *just because?*" I asked.

He looked me in the eye and said, "We have to take care of you, and this is how I'm able to give back."

They left and I left, and that was the end of our initial interaction.

Fast forward a month later. I was applying to the FBI, going through all the transition courses, and nothing stood out. There weren't a lot of opportunities in Virginia Beach where I lived, and I kept looking at Bill's business card.

One day, I thought, *You know what? Why not?*

I got on the phone with him and said, "Hey, Bill. I'm gonna come out and take you up on your offer. I'll come meet your staff and just see what you have to offer because I have nothing to lose."

He said, "Okay, my assistant is going to email you. We're going to give you several dates, so pick a date and come on out."

And that's what I did.

A month later, I flew out to Los Angeles and stayed in Beverly Hills. I met Bill and his staff that Monday morning, and I was anxious and suspicious because I still had no idea—my mind couldn't comprehend—why this gentleman would do all this for a complete stranger. I don't know if the hostility and the anxiety came out, but for me, it was palpable.

Bill came and sat down with a huge smile on his face.

Kent came and said, "Mark, I'm so glad you're here." I could tell by the way he was looking at me and talking to me that he was being genuine.

Bill was so happy for me to be there, and he said, "Mark, I've given this offer multiple times over the last ten years, and you were the only person who's ever taken me up on it."

Then, they both said, "Let's get started."

So we got started.

I met Bill's staff and the people in his circle, and they talked to me as if I was the most important client they had in their portfolio.

Everyone in Bill and Kent's circle were so genuinely kind and excited to find out more about me and help me figure out my next chapter. It was both thrilling and overwhelming at the same time.

My plan was to relax and take a bunch of notes when I got there. Truth be told, I honestly thought that Bill was going to roofie my drink and I was gonna wake up in a tub full of ice with a missing kidney.

At that point, I would be like *I knew it*. I just knew that's what was going to happen.

But none of that happened at all.

He introduced me to so many people and gave me notes on what I did well, what I needed to improve, and a roadmap for figuring out what's next. He was letting me do my thing and letting me talk. But in actuality, he was observing me.

On Wednesday, Bill and I went to UCLA where he had to speak. And he said, "Mark, I'm looking at your resume. This is really good."

Jokingly, I said, "Well, it's about damn time you looked at it. I've been here for three days."

Then, he tells me, "My method is that I want to look at the resume, look at and observe the individual, and see if the resume matches. I don't have much to tell you about your resume because you've captured it all. Unfortunately, I've come to a decision that you're not a commercial real estate guy."

That seemed like a pretty big deal because Bill is the CEO of an international commercial real estate company.

He said, "I would be doing you a huge disservice to stick you behind a desk and have you look at spreadsheets and do commercial real estate. However, you're part of the family now. So if you want a job or need a job, you always have it. I'm gonna send you back home on Friday.

"But in the meantime, I'm going to the University of Southern California to meet with the Dean of the Marshall School of Business, and he asked if you wanted to come meet him."

I was very excited to go to the college campus at USC. So I said, "Yeah, of course, I'll go."

We showed up on campus the next day, and it happened to be graduation week. They were having a huge celebration and students were everywhere. *Everywhere.* The atmosphere was fantastic.

When we parked and got out of the car, there were kids falling off their skateboards and running into each other on bikes, yet it was controlled chaos. And it was so much fun. I could *feel* the vibe of it within my first two steps out of the car.

"Bill, this would be such a great place to work," I told him. And he didn't say anything. I decided not to say another word about it and to just enjoy the campus moment.

We walked around campus, met the dean, and then left. It was the most fun I'd ever had. I fell in love with the campus, its history, and all things USC right away. I had no idea that USC would be my home for the next four years. I flew home the next day, and I thought that was the end of it, that my interactions with Bill were done.

Little did I know, those moments were the beginning of some of the most wonderful but also the most grueling chapters in my life.

25

AN OFFER I COULDN'T REFUSE

I flew back to Virginia, excited about my meeting with Bill. When I got home, life continued as it always had. I was still struggling with the transition and trying to figure out my next move.

My wife wanted me to be an ROTC instructor at one of the local high schools, but I was also applying for the FBI. None of it was working out for me. I wasn't making progress.

The application process for ROTC was progressing, but not quickly enough for me to get selected for the upcoming school year. The FBI was also progressing, but the hiring process was so detailed and involved that it was going to take at least two years for me to get selected.

Even if selected, there was no guarantee that I would stay in Virginia. I wasn't getting any closer to a new career, and retirement was right around the corner.

A couple of weeks later, Bill called with that same infectious enthusiasm in his voice and said, "Hey, Mark. I got everything we talked about for the last two weeks. Forget everything we did. I got you four interviews at USC."

For a minute, I sat there, stunned.

"Well, Bill, when are the interviews?" I asked.

"Oh, they're going to be next Tuesday. And yeah, we got you four interviews. So be ready. If you don't have a suit, go get a suit. And we'll see you in a couple weeks."

"Bill, what am I interviewing for?" I asked.

And he very bluntly said, "Oh, don't worry about it. Just don't suck." And he hung up the phone.

I was sitting there with this phone in my hand. I was just completely still, looking at it, feeling utterly overwhelmed by what had just happened on that call. I decided that I would do what he said. I would get a suit. And I would get a USC-colored tie.

I told myself, *Talk to the family today. I'm going out to Los Angeles for an interview at USC.*

Truth be told, I was just thinking of it all as practice because I hadn't really interviewed before. That was the plan—I would go out there to practice, see what was gonna happen, take some notes, and experience what it was like to have a real professional interview. All of it was outside of my comfort zone.

And then the day came.

That Monday, I flew out and showed up at USC for interview number one with a gentleman named Al in the Office of Development. I walked in, and there was a spread of food, four complete strangers, and an unusual excitement from all of my interviewers. The spread was fantastic, and everybody looked eager to see me, which was a surprise because I only expected to meet with Al.

I sat and talked with the four people on my interview panel. They were asking questions, and I was just telling stories and laughing. The whole thing was very upbeat, and I felt absolutely no pressure because I was just practicing.

About halfway through, Al was like, "Oh my goodness, you haven't eaten yet. We've just been talking your ear off." He prompted me to eat, and I took a bite, but then somebody asked me a question, and I started into another story. That pattern lasted for about an hour.

After that, Al said, "Hey, we've got to get you to your next interview. But I want you to come back when your day is done. We just have to talk real quick. No big deal."

"Okay, no problem."

I was almost giddy about it. It seemed like it went really well. I went on to my next interview, and that also went well. Then I went to my third and my fourth.

In my second interview, that gentleman flat-out told me, "Mark, I would love to have you on my staff. You seem like you'd be a really great fit."

Of course, I shook his hand and said, "Yes, sir. Let me go think things over, but I'll definitely get back to you."

Then, I went back down to talk with Al, and he said, "Hey, Mark, come on in here. Sit down. I've just got something really quick to talk to you about." He looked at me with this giant grin on his face, gave me a huge handshake, and said, "So, what's it going to take to get you to USC?"

I just kind of looked at him, clearly not understanding what he was talking about. And I think he saw that, so he said, "You know, for you to pack up and come on out to LA, what will it take?"

That's when it hit me. *Oh, shit. This is a job offer.*

I was trying to *not* get hired, so I threw out a number that I thought was astronomical. As a kid, I was gonna work for the post office and make $35,000 a year and have a pension. The military isn't much different. But times have changed.

I looked him square in the face with my huge number, and said, "$150,000."

Without blinking, he said, "Oh yeah, okay. No problem."

My first inclination was, *Shit. He said yes like it wasn't a big deal.* I honestly thought he'd say something like, "You little punk. You better get your ass out of my office. We're an institute of higher learning. Nobody gets paid that much. This is bullshit. Get out."

That's what I was hoping for because I was looking for a way out.

When he did *not* give me that reaction, I said, "Well, you know, my wife is an audiologist. She's got a great job. And it'd be way too much to ask for her to move out here on a whim."

Al got on the phone, called a number, and said, "Hey, I have a guy I want to hire. His wife is an audiologist. Do you have any positions at the medical center?"

Naturally, I hadn't researched anything because I wasn't going to get hired. But I soon found out that USC has its own hospital and all the departments that go along with that. So, when Al called, the guy said, "Yeah, we have that department. We can get her some interviews. No problem. Anything for you." Then Al hangs up the phone.

Still not convinced, I said, "Okay, well … I've got three kids, and I don't even know where to live. I don't even know where to look for schools."

He grabbed the phone again.

"Hey, I got a guy I want to hire, and he's got three kids. Do you still have those three scholarships floating around that he can use for a year? Just so he figures things out?" And the guy on the other end said, "Oh, yeah. Anything for you, man. We'll get it all set up."

Al hung up the phone and said, "Okay, so are we good?"

I was out of excuses, and I looked at him, almost defeated. "Yeah. Yeah, we're good. Let me just go home and talk to the boss, and I'll get back to you."

"Don't wait too long. I really want to get you here, and I want to get you here as soon as possible," he said.

It was so unexpected that all I could think to say was, "Okay."

When I went home, I told my family, "Gena, kids, you're not gonna believe this. They offered me a job at $150,000 a year. And, Gena, they can get you interviews at their medical center. And kids, you can go to private school 'til we figure it out. One of the perks is that if I stay there for three years, you guys get to go to USC for free."

All my bases were covered. I was so excited and relieved because at the end of the day, I still needed to provide for my family and everything was there that I needed. It was a brand-new environment. It was a university. And I was pumped.

After telling my wife, she said, "Yeah, I don't want to do that. I want to stay here in Virginia Beach."

In utter disbelief, I said, "Why? Did you hear the deal I just got?"

"Well, I don't like it," she said. "I don't want to do it."

My plan was to call Al and say, "I'm sorry, Al. I'm not going to be able to take the job, but thank you so much for the offer." However, something told me to call Bill first.

I called Bill and said, "Hey, Bill, Al offered me a job, and it's amazing, but Gena refuses to move out to LA for a university job. She gave every excuse in the book for not going."

Bill said, "Just fly out. Have your wife do the interviews. We'll walk around LA a little and get to know the city. Maybe that'll change her mind."

We flew out, and she just refused to budge even an inch. I was incredibly confused. I genuinely thought this was an ideal decision for our family, so I thought she'd be open to this opportunity. (Gena had created her own mosaic of how life was going to be once I retired—and USC and Los Angeles were not part of that mosaic.)

I could understand because it was one more huge move, a move to another different city on the West Coast. We had lived in

California before, so she just absolutely *did not want* to do it, but she still flew out. She looked at it all. And we didn't communicate almost the entire time because she was angry.

We went back home, and I called Bill and said, "Bill, thanks so much for flying us out. I just don't think it's gonna work."

That's when Bill said, "Look. How about this? How about having Gena come back out and she can pick out any house in Los Angeles, even at the beach? Anywhere in the greater Los Angeles area that she wants to live, she can pick a house. I'll give you a low-interest loan. If you stay out here for five years, then the house is yours."

Again, I went back to Gena and said, "You are not going to believe what just happened ..." and told her the offer.

"No, I'm not gonna ... I'm not gonna take it."

At that point, I said, "Look. Something good is going to happen in all of this. I don't know what it is, but I have to take this opportunity. I want you to come with me. I want the kids to come with me. I'm going to take the job offer."

Two hours later, Al called and said, "Hey, Mark. I really want to hire you, and I know that the other gentleman gave you an offer. I want you to work for me."

"Oh, I'd love to, but I already committed to Tom," I said.

"That's fine. I already talked to Tom, and Tom's fine with it. And we're gonna go ahead and start you off at $165,000 a year," he told me.

I laughed at him. "Are you giving me a raise before I even start?!"

He just kind of laughed at me and said, "Well, yes."

And I said, "Okay."

I accepted the offer, packed up my stuff, and started my week-long drive across the country to LA. What a shock to the system that was ...

26

FAILING UPWARD

I was failing upward.

After a twenty-year career, I was struggling through my transition out of the military. Everything about life just felt off. I didn't have a form of therapy that worked well. And I just wasn't myself.

I'd moved to LA and started a new job at the University of Southern California. It was all new. I wasn't doing great, and things were piling up ... I was learning a new job, trying to keep my family together, starting graduate school, and figuring out my new normal as a civilian. I wasn't doing well inside my own skin.

But the one thing that I did have was my ability to get on my bike and ride. When the weekends came, I would head out for a long ride in Pasadena.

Growing up, I always had a bike. From the time that I learned to balance and move forward on those two wheels, I found peace in the pedaling. Riding my bike allowed me to escape into my own world. It was fun, and it was how I processed information.

Taking my bike through neighborhoods, back roads, or mountain trails had become my happy place. It's the way I worked out any emotions I was going through, and it was the closest thing to therapy that I knew.

My bike was my sanctuary.

But Navy life … BUD/S and SEAL training wasn't conducive to cycling. Our workouts revolved around running and swimming. For at least seven years of my service, there was no pedaling.

And that was okay. All the training kept me in top physical condition for two deployments and Officer Candidate School. I was holding up just fine.

But when I deployed to Iraq and returned, it was the first time we were running back-to-back missions with full body armor, often for days at a time. All of that stress on my body wasn't exactly a recipe for healthy joints, so my knees hurt, my feet hurt, my hips hurt. Everything in my lower body hurt.

After I got my check-up, my doc said something funny. "Mark, your 6'2", 220-pound frame is not designed for running, and we're going to have to figure out a way to keep you in shape without running so much. I recommend you buy a bike and ride as your form of physical training."

That made me really happy. I did my research, found a bike, and started riding it. The first time I rode, it felt like I was in a time warp. I was transported back to that kid who used his bike for everything … The wind in my face, legs pumping, and breathing deeply opened the door to a flood of good memories on the back of my bike.

I carried that knowledge with me into my retirement from the SEALs and onto my new career path at USC. It's what made going on long rides in sunny Pasadena such a natural and easy thing for me to do.

Pasadena is this stunningly beautiful place about ten miles north of Los Angeles. Although I grew up across the country in Ohio, I already felt a connection. As an avid Ohio State football fan, I watched the Buckeyes play in the Rose Bowl and never missed a Rose Parade. But I never expected to actually visit.

I lived in Pasadena and rode my bike at the Rose Bowl every weekend. It was great. And it was just what I needed to grind out my frustrations, to figure life out through all these transition points, and to feel something other than anger or disappointment in myself.

My routine was to ride around the Rose Bowl twice and then head north to breathtaking hills and mountains that went on for miles and miles. I could just lose myself in the grandeur and ride until my legs almost fell off and my lungs were on fire. Completely exhausted and completely happy.

However, it was getting harder and harder to find much-needed peace after a ride. And despite the fact that I was regularly seeing a therapist, I was really only comfortable feeling anger or expressing anger. If anything came close to an emotion like sadness or disappointment, my throat would literally begin to close up.

God forbid that I was actually going to shed a tear. So, to side-step those feelings-which-must-be-avoided-at-all-costs, I played defense against my therapist, managing to *not* address what was going on with me mentally. Yet in my mind, I knew that I wasn't going to get better if I just kept running from the emotions that needed to surface in order for me to move forward.

One day, my therapist asked me a question that utterly confused me. We were having a session and something came up about me not doing well, and she said, "Where do you feel this in your body?"

I had no idea what she was talking about.

I mean ... I had *no clue*. My entire body was *always* buzzing—at least, that's what I would call it. I was anxious and kind of angry, and my whole body felt as if every nerve was on fire and at constant attention. I'd gotten to a place where I didn't know any different. This was my normal.

So when she asked me where I felt that in my body, I almost canceled my appointments because I thought, *I don't know what that means. I'm spending all this money trying to get better, and you're asking me where I feel emotions in my body.* I would finish those sessions, hop on my bike, and do the Pasadena ride—which, at the time, seemed to be my best form of therapy.

It was after a session when I found the perfect technical climb, but I'd have to go down a super steep mountain to get to the bottom, immediately turn, and climb up for about an hour. I did my standard two-loop warm-up around the Rose Bowl and then rode up the mountains.

I could often escape and imagine hearing the crowd cheer for Ohio State or USC when I would do my warmup laps around the stadium. The first climb was awesome and just what I needed on that picturesque day in Southern California.

I made it up the long climb and was on my way down the hill that promised a short rest before the grueling ride back up that punished my body to the point of near collapse. I was looking forward to pushing my mind and body after that therapy session. Well, I came to that incredibly sharp descent, and there was a car coming up the hill around the turn.

Imagine speeding down a hill on your bike with a turn waiting for you at the bottom, knowing that there's nothing to slow you down but your brakes. Then, a car comes around that turn, *your turn*, but it's not on the right side of the road. It's encroaching on *your side* of the road.

The driver was oblivious because he was on his phone. He didn't see me barreling down the hill at twenty-five miles per hour. I had a decision to make. I knew that if I kept going forward, I was going to run into his car, and there was no way I would survive. Or, option number two, hit the brakes as hard as I could and attempt the turn, knowing that I was probably going to wreck.

Sure enough, being alive was my favorite thing. Obviously, I chose option number two and hit the brakes. Before I knew it, I was sliding on the ground at twenty-five miles an hour, masterfully skinning the entire right side of my ass. If you've never used asphalt like it was body sandpaper, you may not realize the damage it does.

I was in horrible pain. But I got up, dusted myself off, and checked my bike. My gearing was all torn up, forcing me to limp my bike the four miles back to my apartment. Even after surviving SEALs, I can still say it was probably the most painful, longest four-mile bike ride of my life.

After what seemed like hours, I got to my apartment, looked at the road rash, and it was just nasty. But I knew I had to get it cleaned up, so I hopped in the shower and started to painstakingly remove bits of gravel, spurs, and horribly damaged skin.

If you haven't spent much time in California, you probably don't know the water is harsh as hell. Each drop felt like a razor blade that day. Then I did what any grown man would do. I screamed in agony because the pain was almost unbearable.

I realized that a trip to the hospital was in order. So, I got myself an Uber, made my way to USC Hospital where the staff goes, and talked to the doc. I told him I needed to get this thing taken care of, and he said, "Mark, we don't have an ER here. You're going to have to go to the ER, which is about thirty miles away. Plan to be there for four to six hours, minimum."

Well, that was unacceptable. I asked him what my other options might be. He told me there was a clinic on campus that might be able to take care of me. So I got back in an Uber, went back to campus, and my wound started oozing. It was awful and ridiculously painful.

The doc took a look and said, "It's a pretty good road rash, and you actually did a good job cleaning it up." Then they cleaned up the rest for me, which was excruciating. He gave me gauze and medical supplies to make sure I was taken care of for my two-week trip home to Virginia.

See, I had plans to get home and celebrate my daughter's birthday. My kids' birthdays were (*and still are*) a really big deal to me, and I made sure to never miss a birthday as long as I had life in my body. The next morning, I took a red-eye and suffered my way through the entire flight. I didn't sleep, couldn't get comfortable, and stayed in a continual state of pain.

I landed in Virginia, went to the house, changed the gauze, and picked up Braden, Evan, and Olivia. I took them all to Great Wolf Lodge for the night and watched all the kids have a beautiful time together. Then we woke up and made our way to Busch Gardens.

Of course, when my daughters and son saw me the next morning, they immediately knew something was wrong. But I preached to my kids that I wouldn't break a promise, and I had promised my daughter that I was going to do this birthday with her. There was no way I would cancel our visit to Great Wolf Lodge and Busch Gardens.

Everything was okay. I just stayed off of my injured side as much as possible and limped around so as not to miss a moment. But I wanted to ride at least one of the rides with my kids. As I got in line, my kids just looked at me like, *Dad are you okay?* And I did what dads do and told them I was going to be fine.

My kids were so sweet. They picked a ride where you were pretty much dangling in a seat, so I didn't have to sit down because that would've torn up my leg even more. I got on the ride and they strapped me in.

Well, I thought I might get bumped around a little bit. But I got bumped around at every turn, hit my road rash each time, and I was seriously suffering. Have you ever seen a big black man turn ashy and almost pale? I got off that ride looking like a ghost.

My kids saw it. And in that moment, I faced a choice that seemed like the lesser of two evils. I could focus all of my efforts on the searing physical pain I was experiencing, or I could focus all my energy on the emotional pain that was hovering just beneath the surface.

But I couldn't do both.

The pain from my bike accident was so bad that I almost couldn't function, so I made the conscious choice, thinking, *Okay, physical pain it is.* Then, I told the kids to go on a ride, found a small corner out of the way of all the people, and solely focused on the physical pain.

It was as if this bodily torture had turned into dynamite on the dam that had been holding back the torrent of emotional pain. Suddenly, everything other than anger came rushing. It was disappointment. It was confusion. It was feeling like I wasn't enough, like I wasn't good at anything.

That emotional toll completely overwhelmed me because I'd never come to the point where I had to choose what to focus on. And I was very inexperienced at dealing with an emotional onslaught. So I just lay down and slowly curled up until I'd pulled myself into something like the fetal position.

And I finally cried.

I cried because ...

I never cried when my father died or at his funeral.

I never cried when I lost my dear friend and teammate.

I never cried when my cousin died in a car crash at only twenty-nine years old.

I never cried at losing friends and teammates to either combat or suicide.

I never cried at the countless other incidents that normally would have invoked tears.

My tears had been bottled up, packed away, and kept under strict lock and key because there is no room for crying in my line of work … absolutely no exceptions!

The tears forced their way past every barrier I'd so carefully constructed. Every part of me ached with those tears. My body was heaving from the sobs that refused to be held by that dam. And it was the most embarrassing moment of my entire life because I never thought that I was capable of experiencing the level of despair that had been locked up in my body.

I just laid there in a dark corner, curled up on myself, and my body was shaking. I was shaking so hard that I was almost convulsing. Though it was probably only twenty minutes, it felt like I'd been there for twelve hours.

I finished out the day with my kids, aware that I couldn't go on like this. I had to *choose* to get better. And had I not had that degree of physical and mental pain to deal with, then I wouldn't have taken the time or made the effort to get better.

My bike crash was the catalyst for my unavoidable wake-up call to stop fighting this monster. The way I dealt with emotional trauma during my time in SEAL Teams wasn't working for me anymore …

My team support system was gone.

My expertise no longer applied.

My reputation, my status, my prestige … had all vanished.

I was just some guy named Mark Greene working at USC and failing upward.

But there was no doubt in my mind that I had to get better. That crash caused me to become unsealed, which led to the realization that I needed help.

When I got back to California and had a session with my therapist, I was telling her about the crash and the breakthrough that I had. I told her to ask me again where I feel it in my body. She asked again, and for the first time, I knew that I felt it in my chest. It was the oddest sensation to feel things when my whole body wasn't lit up.

I noticed that I had to concentrate on where the anger was sitting. My chest hurt, but not in a way I can describe. It wasn't quite physically painful, yet I could feel it deep inside.

I knew I couldn't get to it on my own, so that's when I fessed up to my therapist. I said, "I figured out a way to play defense against you, and I've been doing it for about six months. Whenever you ask me something emotional, I would redirect and ask you a question that I knew you were interested in. You would completely answer my question and forget about the emotional subject that you were working toward."

And I said, "Whenever I do that, you have to stop me because I'm fighting against you to keep you from reaching deep down and starting work on this emotional side of things." That was all she needed to hear from me to make an adjustment in her therapy.

Once I reached that place, the change in my healing process was exponential. It was the pivotal moment for moving forward in my journey to better emotional and mental health.

I had to face *all* of myself in order to successfully step into the transition process. Up to that time, I'd only been putting Band-Aids on gaping wounds. I didn't want to take a long, hard look at them. I didn't want to sign up for the emotional surgery that I needed.

27

INVISIBLE INJURIES

When I retired and got out of teams, I experienced one of my hardest transition points. I'd lost my "Locker Room." And to a degree, I lost my identity, I lost my purpose, and I lost my tribe.

One of the starkest realities is that once you leave that environment—once you leave that locker room—it's impossible to recreate it. And when you go back into that community, you are tolerated but not welcomed.

This is how the military is designed for the service members to thrive and continue its mission—without veterans or retirees being part of it. They have new SEALs coming in every day to replace the people who are leaving.

So when you want to go back and try to stay connected, the guys you were in platoons with and deployed with, they're still doing the job. *They're still busy.* They're still on training trips, and they have a few minutes for you, or they might be able to join you for a beer.

But for the most part, you are no longer a part of the team. *I* wasn't part of a team. And that was really hard to digest.

You can't successfully thrive in the military community without putting your heart and soul and sacrifices into it. When you lose that, it's a really significant loss. It feels as if you've lost a piece of your heart, your core identity.

And another thing happened when I retired.

On a Friday, I was a member of an elite Special Operations team. But by Saturday, I was just regular, run-of-the-mill Mark Greene. When you make that transition, the hardest thing to come to grips with is that you're no longer special …

You're no longer part of that elite community. You're just a guy. And if you do it the right way, you're going to continue to thrive. But if you don't, you're going to flounder.

In every fiber of my being, I felt that. I needed community. I needed to know who I was without SEALs.

It ultimately comes down to how fast you can recover and, hopefully, find another tribe again. Luckily, I found a tribe at USC, but it came with significant costs.

When I first showed up at USC, I didn't know what my invisible injuries were. I was so busy and so focused, driving and striving toward perfection and maintaining my skill set that the noise buzzing in the background was masked because I stayed busy.

But what happens in the absence of noise?

When you don't have that noise, when you don't have that environment to go work in every day, when you're not working at that intense level, all of those small—or even large and visible—injuries start to manifest. As I began to settle in at USC, I could finally feel the magnitude of my cognitive injuries.

I was not myself.

Problems and situations that I normally solved quickly had begun to decline rapidly. I often stopped what I was doing because I either couldn't figure out how to do something or what I was thinking became permanently lost … and I had no idea what was going on or how to fix it.

My ability to instantaneously solve complex problems was replaced by a lot of anxiety, sleepless nights, and continuous mental reel replaying my life and my time in the team's good, bad, and ugly. It was grueling and it followed me, clinging to my thoughts.

I didn't know how to adjust to losing my capacity for critical thinking or the nearly complete loss of self and identity. And with that loss of problem-solving and my sense of self, I was also losing my biggest attribute—my ability to think outside the box.

Being creative in thinking and doing this very dynamic job, the smallest tasks of paying rent on time, setting up a schedule, and trying to learn a new city had me on complete overload. To make matters worse, I didn't have a car. I was commuting by train every day.

I was learning a new job in a new city where there were no SEALs anywhere. There were no guns anywhere, there was no urgency anywhere. And I just had to sit with my deteriorating condition and hope for the best.

I was attempting to figure out so many new things on my own. I was still learning my way around my new home and workplace.

And I was walking through the quad on campus when I experienced my first case of turmoil, and my old life and training kicked in along with the muscle memory ...

I was heading into a building to get lunch. I ended up talking to somebody I'd recently met, and the conversation went longer than I planned. The campus was pretty empty because people were in classes. It was quiet.

Well, I turned the corner while talking to my friend Jake, expecting to see an empty campus, but I saw a campus full of people. All of a sudden, I felt claustrophobic and was back in enemy territory.

As a sniper for seventeen years of my career, I saw everything as a target. Standing there with Jake, I instantly saw targets everywhere. My mind was on high alert.

Everything is a danger.

I can't protect myself.

I can't protect Jake.

I didn't have my teammates with me as support while addressing this new threat. And instead of acting as I had for twenty years, I was frozen. My mind and body were screaming to handle this new threat the same way I had thousands of times in the past.

Jake looked at me and asked, "Hey, man, are you okay?" His voice snapped me out of it.

I came to and said, "Yeah, yeah, I'm fine."

He said, "Whoa, what just happened?"

"I don't know … I don't know," I said.

"What did you see? You had this look of anxiety. And you went from Mark Greene, a normal guy who walks around a college campus in a suit to 'Holy shit, I'm in danger. There are targets everywhere. And I have to escape,'" he said.

That's when I came to the realization that I needed help. Because I was *not* myself. I was not the self I'd known for twenty years. And I wasn't able to thrive because I just *could not adjust* to this new docile environment.

For twenty years, I operated at an intensity level between an eight and a ten. And being on a college campus, I was between a one and a two. But when you're used to existing and thriving at an eight to ten and everything's a threat, you're at a loss for what to do when the biggest threat is a kid on a skateboard.

Out of the blue, that "skateboard" became my ten. And I went into the virtue of the training that I had for so long and the combat experiences that I had.

It brought to the forefront that there were some seriously devastating things going on with my psyche, my mental health, and my physical health that I just couldn't deal with on my own. Fortunately, being on a college campus meant that there was a ton of help available to the staff. I decided to talk to somebody I trusted and let them know that I wasn't okay.

Every day I struggled because I wasn't sure that I was going to be able to live up to my potential because I just couldn't figure out this new life. And although I was in a great environment, I was still struggling.

I didn't have any direction. I didn't know where to go. I didn't have an established support system. I was starting from scratch.

Like I said, LA is one of the biggest cities in the world and USC is one of the biggest universities in the country. I was absolutely overwhelmed, and I felt like I wanted to crawl into a dark corner, get in the fetal position, and hope for this one to pass.

And unfortunately, it just got worse.

28

A NEW HOME AND
A BROKEN ONE

In a city as vast as Los Angeles, if you try to take it all in as a whole, you're going to get in way over your head quickly. However, if you're able to take the city in as several small slices, then over time you'll get to see what an amazing city LA can be.

For me, I wasn't in the entertainment industry, and I wasn't in the "Rat Race" to be the next big thing in LA. I was happy being Mark Greene, who happened to be a former Navy SEAL, happily working at USC.

Pasadena was the perfect place for me to land and begin my journey of discovering and growing to love LA. Pasadena was originally settled by people from the Midwest and it still somehow kept its Midwestern roots about it and it didn't quite feel like LA. It felt more like LA lite, and since it was so far from the city, it made it the ideal pace for me to make my transition from tolerating LA to growing to absolutely love it.

One of my fondest memories during my arrival at USC and being on campus for the first couple of weeks is how fanatical USC Trojans are about just *being* at USC. When I'd visited the campus six months prior, it was so festive, one big party and everyone was rabid about being a USC Trojan.

The campus has a warm, welcoming vibe. I knew I was in the right place. And I knew it was *my* place.

I knew that I had to recover from different things due to my time in service. I was looking for a tribe. And USC was the best tribe that I could be a part of.

So one day, I was attending a mandatory tailgate event before the USC football game. I'd never been to a USC game. I'd been to college, and I'd played sports, but I'd never been to a tailgate like this.

I got to campus early because we needed to be there to prepare the event for the alumni and donors. There were a few students walking around or riding skateboards, but nothing unusual compared to what I'd experienced before.

However, as the day progressed, there was this sea of red shirts and hats, and the celebration of USC football. The band (which is world famous) played a little concert in different parts of campus, and I happened to be on a part of the campus where the concert first started.

I heard the drums in the background, and then the USC band came. Everybody had sunglasses on. They were just happy to be in the band and performing. I just sat there in awe, feeling like a kid again.

Everything about game day was such a celebration, and I looked around and everybody was so happy to celebrate all things USC.

As far as the eye could see, there were people draped in cardinal and gold singing the USC fight song and having an absolute blast. People of all ages were immersed in it ... Some were seven years old, and some were seventy, sitting next to freshmen and former students ... And every one of them was excited about the USC celebration happening mere feet from me and the other Trojans.

They played their concert, and I was talking with people around me.

"When did you graduate?" they asked.

"Oh, no. I'm new here. I only started working two weeks ago, and this is my first game. I'm not a Trojan yet."

"Oh, no, no, no. You work here. You're a Trojan." Then they wrapped their arms around me.

My goal is for everyone to get to know me as Mark, so as the conversation got a little deeper, I wanted them to not only meet me but also get to know me. I wanted them to walk away thinking, *Oh, what a nice young man.* And find out later that the nice young man used to be a Navy SEAL.

When I told people that I'd recently started working there and apologized for not being a Trojan, they didn't care about any of that. They were happy that I was there. They were happy that I'd chosen to come work at USC and told me I was going to be a great fit, and they know it.

I immediately went from floundering and deeply mourning the loss of my SEAL Team to knowing that I have my new tribe. And I was so excited. I felt like a kid who'd gone to his first important football game or sporting event *ever.*

I loved how accepting, kind, and jovial the USC Trojans were about their campus, their school, their legacy, and their history.

At that moment, I said to myself, *I have to find a way to be here and make USC a part of my life forever.* But I didn't know how I was going to do that since I was still commuting from Los Angeles to Virginia, trying to keep my family together, and not doing great at any one thing.

Meanwhile, all my invisible injuries were starting to manifest more and more as I wasn't sleeping more than four hours a night. I was too worried about my family back home, going through the guilt of moving cross country to pursue this next chapter, and simultaneously mourning the absence of my family. I wanted them to be a part of it and join me on this new journey to this weird place that I was quickly growing to love.

So when I had that amazing feeling at USC, it was tainted and incomplete. I had wanted my kids to experience this new thing that I'd found and all these people that were there to help. I knew it was the right decision, but I was also deeply saddened that they weren't going to be a part of it with me, or part of this new discovery process and the struggles of figuring it out.

All the emotions, confusion, and self-doubt that you go through in any transition period from kindergarten to first grade, junior high to high school, high school to college, joining the military— everybody experiences change. And all changes have one thing in common: They're difficult. They're manageable, but you have to make the effort to make the transition a good one.

Well, I was lucky, and my transition point was at a place where there was help available. Even though it was a very big city and a very big place, everything I needed was at the place I worked. And I loved the place where I worked.

I enjoyed my job, but I was brand new at fundraising. It was completely unfamiliar territory. I know I'm not quite good at it, but I know that I have the skills to do it.

At that point, I had to be proactive in managing all the chaos that was going on internally. I had to present as being calm, even though at some points, I was panicking, suffering, and disoriented by so many new things to learn, so many new things happening around me.

I was like a walking, open wound of loss on many counts ... So, at the moment when the band came through and I was doing the USC fight-on salute, I realized that I was part of this wonderful community with no needed qualifiers other than my presence. There was a sense of camaraderie and everybody was on the same team.

And along with that came the confidence that I was exactly where I was meant to be.

Next, I tried to figure out how to transition in a way that helped me stay productive, helped me keep my family together, and also addressed what once started as a small echo in my life—my cognitive decline. Those injuries had reached max volume in my body and brain.

I was utterly overwhelmed by that transition process. I just couldn't get a grip on it. And what I didn't yet understand was my depth of sadness and that I was mourning the loss of my career.

Although I'd never intended to make "the SEAL Teams" and "being a SEAL" my identity, after twenty years, it was bound to happen.

The things I complained about the most, I found out I really loved the most. I loved competing at a high level, I loved getting better every day, and I loved the competition with my teammates.

There was a significant void with that transition. Although I was wrestling in the midst of the void, I was in an environment where I knew I could get the help I needed.

However, I still needed to solve the problem of keeping my family together. That brings us to another transition: the change in my marital status from married to divorced. I learned pretty quickly that I wasn't going to be able to hold on to my marriage. But as a SEAL, I would never quit. I would never give up on the hope of keeping my marriage and family together. Quitting was not in my vocabulary.

So I did what was necessary and asked if I could commute two weeks—two weeks on campus and a week back in Virginia to at least try to keep things together. Yet, the decision was out of my hands because no matter how much effort I put toward fixing the marriage, my wife and I couldn't find the same page to continue our story together.

All of that slowly led to my divorce, and again, I found myself in another state of change. It seemed as if I was constantly in a transitioning freefall. I became increasingly aware that I wasn't even doing well in the parts of my transition that I needed to quickly get a handle on.

Over the course of the next year, I continued to spiral downward … until one day it all culminated in a department store.

29

HOME DEPOT DILEMMA

Despite my best efforts, my marriage was falling apart and my spouse filed for divorce. I left my house because I was bought out of my portion. I was trying to formulate a plan for what to do next to remain in the lives of my children and continue to be an involved father.

I made the very conscious decision that although I was no longer going to be married, I was going to be in the lives of my kids. In order to do that, I had to commute. And in my mind, I knew that I'd eventually move back to Virginia because the USC transition was supposed to be temporary.

Even though we were in the middle of a divorce and no longer sharing a home, I still wanted to live in the same neighborhood. My mentality was that I wanted my kids to be free to come to my house and see me whenever they wanted to.

I began looking for houses in the same neighborhood, and there were several available. A perfect house was only ten houses away, and my kids could walk to my house at any time, day or night.

My ex didn't like that, but she was no longer part of the equation. It wasn't about my divorce, it was about being the best father to my kids.

One day, I took my girls with me to Home Depot. I had to move in a frantic rush because I'd just received half of the money from our house, bought my new house, and needed to furnish the place in a single weekend.

I was at Home Depot with two of my daughters buying blinds, and I had all the notes and measurements in my trusty Team Guy notebook. I'd taken all the measurements of the blinds, and I had written down the number that I needed. It was all in my book, and everything was gonna be simple.

As we walked around, I told them what I was doing. I picked up the blinds that I wanted. Looking at my list, I realized there were a couple of things missing. I looked at the shelf, I looked at my list, and I couldn't figure out the problem.

I didn't know what I was doing wrong, so I took everything out and went through the checklist again. I had to do it at least ten times, and each time, my daughter was watching. *There's no way I can't solve this problem.*

Yet, the more I looked at it, the worse it got.

I started thinking back to how sharp I used to be. I remembered how I could make calculations instantly or take a sniper shot. I had to think on my feet because everything moves so quickly, from the training to the battlefield.

Yet there I stood, looking at this very simple checklist. There was no way for me to solve this problem. My daughter came up, grabbed my hand, and grabbed the notebook. We put everything back, and then we counted each item one by one. She looked at it within the cart and checked it off.

By that time, she was really scared. She could tell that her daddy wasn't the same as he used to be. This very simple problem was something he couldn't handle. And she looked at me, tears beginning to roll, and asked, "Daddy, are you okay?"

The sparkle had left my eyes. The laughter was gone. The way we connected through music was a distant memory. She saw that I was struggling to the point of utter collapse.

I looked at her and said, "No. I can't solve this problem, and I need your help."

She helped me, and we made it out of Home Depot.

Had she and Livi not been there to save me, I'd still be stuck in that aisle trying to figure out how to solve the basic problem of putting shades for my house in the cart. The amount of effort it took to do such a simple task … I just couldn't get it done. There was no way I could tackle that basic problem.

Cognitively and emotionally, I knew I wasn't the same person. But I didn't see a way that I could survive. I was starting to feel that I'd become a burden because I couldn't keep my marriage or my family together.

Add to that the fact that I couldn't perform at the level that I had for two decades. I was no longer good at any one thing. It'd become painfully obvious that the help that I was getting through finding my tribe and working wasn't enough, even though I loved it.

I needed so much more help than I realized, and I didn't know where to start. I didn't know what modalities were out there. And I didn't even know how it was gonna get better. So, I fell into this unusual place of feeling incompetent.

I call it being consciously incompetent, which means I sucked and I knew it, and I needed my 10-year-old to help solve what felt like quantum physics.

That spurred me on to do the research, and I soon realized that the traditional therapies weren't working. I wasn't getting to the root of my cognitive downward spiral, and I needed to do something that would get me better because I couldn't see a way out of this rapid decline. I knew my time to start the healing process was limited.

I started to understand that post-traumatic stress was different than I thought. It manifests differently in different people. And with the SEAL Teams, your decline is slower because you're still functioning at a high level and you're still able to do the work. I don't know if it's muscle memory or that you're on autopilot with so much of it …

But even then I knew that post-traumatic stress was an issue and that my traumatic brain injuries were real. And they were having a very real effect on me.

Like I said, I had a very limited window to get this problem solved. And I did what so many SEALs do when we are struggling with something—pile more things on to help in our work environment because we just stay busy.

In the SEALs, you don't have to look at where you are deficient or where you are having problems. You have your teammates and everybody's kind of going through the same thing. You just rally around each other. The mission is all-important.

Once I realized that even though I was in a good place location-wise and work-wise, I no longer had a mission, I no longer had a goal to achieve. So I made it my goal to get better.

But before I could get better, I learned there was one more thing that nobody should do when you're in the middle of a fight. Never try to fight the enemy on your own or without a plan.

The feeling that settled into my gut as my daughters watched me struggle is something I'm not sure I can accurately describe. Fear, shame, and anxiety—those are just a few of the words that come to mind.

I will never forget the look in my daughters' eyes as they watched their daddy struggling to do simple math. They knew something wasn't okay.

And that look, that feeling of helplessness was the final straw for me to realize I had to get help.

30

PICKING UP THE PIECES

Most of the help I received after transitioning to civilian life came from my time at USC. That place captured my heart, and I knew I wanted to be a Trojan forever.

While I was there, I had the opportunity to apply for grad school. But that was when I was working full time, and I could get four hours per semester at no cost. I applied, went through the process, and got accepted.

That was right when I decided to move back to Virginia to be close to my kids since their mom and I were no longer going to be living under the same roof. Once I moved from working full time to part time, I would lose the benefit, and I couldn't afford tuition.

It looked like my dream of being a Trojan wasn't going to be realized before I had to leave. So I called my mentor, and I said, "Bill, I've got great news."

And he wanted me to meet him for lunch to tell him my news in person. I went to his office in Beverly Hills to meet him, and I was so excited. "Bill, you're not going to believe it," I said, "but I got into USC." He was genuinely thrilled for me and had the biggest smile on his face.

"But Bill, unfortunately, I'm not going to be able to take the classes and start school because I went to part-time and I just don't have the money."

Just like always, he got on the phone and called Kent to tell him the good news. He asked Kent if the company still had scholarships for veterans and Kent replied, "Yeah, Bill, we still have a scholarship left."

And Bill said, "Well, Mark got into USC, and we're gonna go ahead and give him the scholarship because he went to part-time. He wants to be a Trojan, and this is his opportunity. So we have to make that happen."

And Kent said, "Bill, it'll be done by this afternoon."

Bill hung up the phone, looked at me with the pride of a father, and said, "No son of mine is paying for school."

And he took care of the bill for me to go to USC. That level of kindness was something I had never experienced. And Bill was the one who facilitated my coming out to Los Angeles in the first place.

He looked at me and said, "We got you in school. So you gotta get straight A's."

I was so proud and determined that I promised them I'd get straight A's.

So fast forward. School was starting.

When I'd previously attended grad school, it was a different program in the military. It was still very challenging, but there were a lot of resources, and the pace was conducive to success. The Naval Postgraduate School was designed for military service members who'd been out of school for a while to go through the paces slower until getting used to going back to school before ramping up.

However, the USC graduate program is a Top 20 University. The program I was going to is the Master of Public Policy (MPP), and it was ranked among the top three in the nation. I quickly found that the difference between normal universities and universities in the top percentile was pace and volume.

The pace and volume of USC was intense. I rapidly fell behind. I finished my first semester, but I didn't do well. And I felt terrible because I just kept thinking about the generosity of Bill and that I didn't keep my promise to get straight A's.

I was not getting straight A's. I was going through a divorce. I was down to part time, and even doing part time, I wasn't doing well at work. I just had too many different things going on.

And I was still transitioning.

And I still had all the symptoms of a traumatic brain injury and post-traumatic stress.

And I realized that I was now a burden.

I wasn't doing anything well. I started to wonder if I was good enough or valued enough to stay around.

One day, I was in a really low spot. I was sitting in my apartment lamenting because I was failing. It had been a long, long time since

I flat-out failed at anything. But I had this wonderful friend who I met the first week of school.

She'd had a really hard time, too. And she'd become an anchor for what I was wading through. Her experiences had given her a passion for veterans and veteran support, and she truly understood some of the problems that veterans face.

I was sitting on my bed, feeling the weight of my burden, and I felt myself starting to spiral. (If you've ever spiraled, you know it never leads anywhere good.) So I gave my friend a call and said, "I need you to come over to the house. I have guns here, and I need you to just come over."

I had enough presence of mind to leave the house and walk around the block because I knew it would take about thirty minutes for her to get to me. I finished my walk, and sure enough, thirty minutes later, she came to the house and walked upstairs.

I opened the door and she could see the anguish on my face. She immediately knew I wasn't myself and I was struggling. Suicide hit close to home for her because she'd attempted it, so she knew exactly what was staring her in the face. She knew what I was feeling and what I was going through.

She asked if I was okay and I said, "Um, I will be. I just need the guns out of the house."

When she walked through the door, I was ready. I handed the guns to her and she gave me a hug, looked at me, and said, "You're gonna be okay. We all care about you, and you're valuable."

Then she asked if I needed anything else, and I told her, "I just need to think about the things that are important—about being there for my kids, being available."

And I must pass through what I knew in my mind was a very short phase, because with all the thoughts going through my head, the prevailing thought was that I needed to be there for my kids. What I was going through was very temporary, and I had the one person that I needed at that moment to reconfirm that.

Throughout life and throughout my transitions, I have always had these wonderful people in my life that are put there very strategically and just want what's best for me. And that one intervention in those five minutes, her presence and words to me were invaluable.

Those are some of the best friends I've had—even outside of the teams. The team experience is different from my experience at USC. Through that intervention, I started to have a transition toward good things happening.

But ...

At the back of my mind, I still knew it was time to go soon. So I had a new zeal, and I started to start to thrive again. I'd figured out my job, and I'd talked to vice president Al who'd hired me.

He called me into his office, but I didn't know why. He called me in and apologized to me, saying, "Mark, I have done you a huge disservice by putting you in fundraising. Your light is so bright, and I can't go anywhere on this campus without somebody saying wonderful things about you. I wanted to get you here at USC so badly that this was the only job I could give you to get you here. But now that I see the impact that you've had, tell me what you really want to do."

"I would love to work with the Provost Office on veterans programs," I said. "I'm really passionate about veterans' programs, especially with transitions."

"Are you sure that's what you want to do?" he asked.

I said, "Yes."

By switching over to that position, I became confident that I could provide an invaluable service to the university. That same afternoon, he switched me from working in fundraising to working in the Provost Office.

That was the final step in my transition.

I began working for a program that I could thrive in and make a difference for the veteran community. It was truly when my passion for transitions started, and how I learned that transitions not only affect the service member, but they also affect the entire amily. I knew I could do a lot of good for transitioning veterans who came to USC going through the same things I was going through.

To have somebody in the office available all the time to listen to their issues, connect with them, and let them know that they're not alone was vital. I've had those people in my life, and I wouldn't feel complete or contribute as much as I was unless I was able to give back and provide help and services to the new class of veterans who were transitioning and struggling through it.

Even in the midst of all my own personal struggles, I was getting the help I needed. I was starting to thrive again. Life was moving forward.

31

CONTENDING WITH CHANGE

"Each of us must confront our own fears, must come face to face with them. How we handle our fears will determine where we go with the rest of our lives. To experience adventure or to be limited by the fear of it."

—Judy Blume

At that moment, in front of a total stranger, I felt safe.

Safety is not something I ever experienced when the looming terror of massive change was just over the emotional horizon. What I normally felt was tightness in my chest. Not chest pains that felt like I was in danger of a heart attack, but the dull ache that your body instinctively experiences when danger is near.

The dull ache was accompanied by my reliable companions of sweaty palms and heartbeats that you see shake your entire body with their intensity. In instances that became ever increasing was how my ears would clog up as if I'm on a scuba dive and need to

Valsalva or when on an airplane and your ears won't clear because you're congested.

All of these symptoms hit at different times and at different intensities. No matter the time or intensity, these symptoms are your body's way of screaming for you to fix this problem. However, most of us are unaware that there is even a problem, let alone how to solve it.

When I was about two years away from retirement, the signs that something was wrong was background noise that was distant and barely noticeable. With each passing month toward the inevitable, the volume increased with each symptom until that day in January in New York City, where the volume and intensity finally reached its crescendo and I blurted out, "I'm terrified," to a complete stranger.

I was so honest because I did not think I'd see this nice gentleman ever again, so… *What the hell? Tell the man the truth.*

As a SEAL, I had felt like an impenetrable fortress on a fortified island. I was at the top of my game, with the strength and resilience of the special operations community. I was prepared for every circumstance and faced every challenge head-on with barely a flinch often while being shot at.

However, as I faced retirement, my fortress was replaced by a one-man life raft that had seen better days and was held together by bubble gum and dental floss. My island was replaced by an angry and tumultuous ocean that was cold and unforgiving. I was at the mercy of the ocean in which I was adrift without a motor, sail, rudder, or compass.

Although my teammates were always supportive, they were supportive in the way Team Guys are supportive. Firm handshake with the assurance that, "You're good, dude. Everything is going to be good." Which was basically the blind leading the blind, since leaving the service had not been experienced by me or any of my active teammates. I am forever grateful for their support because they were all in my corner and all were willing to help.

Since my spouse was not able to support me in the time leading up to my retirement and through my civilian transition, most of my emotional support came from my best friend, Ryan. Ryan and I have been friends since we were freshmen in college and have been closer than brothers for over thirty-five years.

That level of closeness is the most valuable relationship that I have outside of my immediate family and my wonderful children. Through every celebration, triumph, setback, and combat deployment, he has been the one constant, and he was unwavering in his support and friendship regardless of the situation.

But my favorite story to tell is when I stumbled into Bill and Kent and found safety and support where I least expected it. As I write this book, I've often wondered why this stranger got such an honest and impulsive answer from me. The reason is they provided me with a sense of nonjudgmental understanding and sincere care for what I was going through.

The time it took me to fully integrate back into the real world and feel like I was back to what I remember as normal took roughly six years to complete. And throughout that process, I experienced uncomfortable changes multiple times.

I transitioned from military to civilian, professional soldier/sailor to professional fundraiser, and professional staff member at a university to full-time student again, combined with the struggles of being married to being divorced.

And finally, after all this time and suffering through traumatic brain injuries, post-traumatic stress, and a lot of the invisible injuries, I've reached the point where I feel like my military transition is complete. Part of that is due to getting the help I needed through typical therapy, Eye Movement Desensitization Reprocessing (EMDR), neurofeedback, the Brain Treatment Center, and just a lot of love and kindness from people who genuinely care about me.

I can tell you without reservation that I no longer battle life's changes. I don't battle my trauma or post-traumatic stress. I'm no longer losing the battle with my TBI and PTS. Now I *contend with them*. And what I mean is that previously, it was an all-out fight that I wasn't prepared to engage in.

I didn't have the necessary tools. I didn't have the motivation. And a lot of times, I didn't have the knowledge. I was fighting against all three of those things as well as my invisible injuries.

For a long time, I was getting my ass kicked because I didn't know how to prepare. I wasn't ready for the all-out fight that some of those injuries forced into my life.

Through a lot of healing, a lot of time, and a lot of the ups and downs of major life changes, I've since gained the necessary tools, motivation, and knowledge. I've learned how to train properly. Instead of approaching change as if I'm about to fight Mike Tyson in his prime, I'm now able to contend with what I'm going through.

Occasionally, I'll take a punch here and a punch there, but now I can punch back and look at the battlefield as being part of my continuous recovery because I can engage with it. It's a back-and-forth.

It's not just me sitting here, waiting for the beating to happen and hoping I survive. I know what I'm doing. I can see what's coming next.

And I can plan how I'm going to contend with post-traumatic stress when it rears its ugly head when I'm in a bit of a mental fog due to my traumatic brain injuries, how I contend with relationships, and how I contend with being a better father.

It's been an incredible journey.

There have been more highs than lows, now that I look back at it. But man, the lows have been exceptionally low. And if I didn't have such a remarkable support system, the lows might've worn me out. But with all the support that I've had, I've come out on top of this.

It started with acknowledging that I needed help and acknowledging it to the right people who have the ability to support me on this journey. I couldn't have done it without them. I am eternally grateful because the people who came into my life after I retired are some of the most wonderful people I've ever met.

So when you're in the middle of the internal chaos of any significant change, and somebody asks if you're okay, *tell them the truth*. Tell them you're not okay. Tell them you need help.

In my situation, when I met the people who influenced me the most and supported me the most, they asked me how I felt. I told Bill that I was scared. And when I would talk to a therapist, I didn't understand what I was going through and I needed help.

I sought out different treatments. And I sought out different modalities of treatment because I wanted to get better. I wanted to be around and enjoy life for the forty-or-so years to come after my time in the military, when this chapter becomes a distant and fond memory.

For the most part, the people out there who asked how I was doing genuinely wanted to help. And depending on your environment, the people who ask often have the ability, the means, and the reach to support you throughout your reintegration process.

Most likely, you're going to need a lot of people to support you. You can't do it on your own—especially if you're in the military. You've been part of a team for your entire length of service, and those do-it-on-your-own muscles have atrophied.

You have the ability, you just need to rediscover it and embrace your metamorphosis.

You have some things to rediscover … rediscover what you like, what you don't like, where you want to live, and what you want to do. And then, you can plan the next phase of your fruitful and exceptional life.

As meticulously as you plan for your military career, your athletic career, or your academic career—*plan your life*.

Major life changes require a lot of preparation and perseverance. You'll experience ups and downs. They're inevitable. But if you stay the course, you *will* come out the other side. And that's where you'll find a new and even better version of you.

If there's one thing I've learned from each of the changes in my life, it's this: transition is temporary.

32

THE TRANSITION CYCLE

"The best way out is always through."

—Robert Frost

As with many things in life, no matter how well you plan an event, party, wedding, childbirth, or mission, the adversary has a say in the outcome. In the case of transition and change, things happening in real time and real life are the unflinching adversary that needs to get transformed from barriers to obstacles.

As I recall my multitude of transitions, they happen in more of a circle that gets revisited or repeated each time I experienced or endured a transition or significant change. Not something you can see or necessarily plan for but must be overcome regardless if you can see around the curve of the circle or not.

For me, when I was transitioning from husband to father, I felt all kinds of things. First, there was the joy of becoming a father, followed almost immediately by the realization that being a father is not something I'd ever done.

I had witnessed parenthood, but never had a child of my own. Someone else's child always goes back to their parents when I was done holding them, or they pooped their diaper, cried too much, or were too much for me to handle with my very limited experience. Certainly not the case with a child of my own. When they pooped, I changed the diaper. When they cried too much, I had to comfort them for sometimes hours at a time. When they were too much for me to handle, *Tough shit*, I thought, *this kid is yours*.

Next came the exploration phase, where I would find out as much information as I could to identify the problem and come up with a solution. Then, I would practice what I learned and worked as hard as I could to master it.

Finally, I became comfortable in my abilities because, although I had not been a father before, I had a ton of untapped or unrealized abilities that simply needed the right spark or situation to bring out the skills that I thought were either dormant or nonexistent.

Each of my transitions followed a similar path. Joy, Realization (or as I like to call panic), Exploration, Practice, and Certainty/Resolution. In the SEAL Teams, we experienced it as Crawl, Walk, Run. We applied this method to everything we did, from diving, shooting, mission prep, skydiving, etc., and it brought us tremendous success and how I try to approach challenges in my life outside of the Teams.

The Six Phases

While discussing my life transitions with a very wise woman, I realized I needed to articulate this metamorphosis into predictable phases. I wanted to explain it in a way that would resonate with you as you navigate the significant changes in your own life.

As with so many things in life that require a "Deep Dive," I needed help, and out of nowhere, someone came to my rescue to support what I feel is the most important part of this book.

I was stuck, trying to frame my transition in ways that are linear with set points that you can see coming or anticipate when you move from one phase to the next. But as you read this, please understand that this is my process, and each person experiences transition differently depending on their background, what they're transitioning from or transitioning to, and how much time you have to explore each phase of this cycle.

I experienced the six phases as Isolation, Indulgence, Cocooning, Emergence, Resolution, and Grief. Let me explain …

Isolation

Since I am an introvert, I process information best when I'm alone with my thoughts. Isolation allows me to work through the big muscle movements as well as the minutia at my own pace. I go to the gym at least four times a week and do yoga.

I still try to squeeze in a bike ride, as riding has been my most trusted therapist since its discovery when I was six. The mind/muscle connection allows me to do a deep dive on whatever situation presents itself and allows me to solve the problem in a way that makes sense to me. It's also how my mind processes complex information.

Isolation is the calm before the storm that is Indulgence.

Indulgence

Indulgence is defined as an occasion when you allow yourself to have something enjoyable, especially more than is good for you.

When I began my transition process after I isolated myself to determine where I wanted to live, what I wanted to do, and the professions that met my criteria, I completely immersed myself in gathering information.

I gorged myself on information. Charts, graphs, demographics, salary, salary specific to that profession, organizational research, employee satisfaction, personal satisfaction, longevity were but a few of the deep-dive sessions I conducted while attempting to figure out this "Transition Thing" that I was desperately trying to avoid, but needed to face head-on, as there was no escape.

Cocooning

Once my gorging and indulgence was over, I needed to develop a cocoon that would allow me to start the metamorphosis from elite warrior, to my new self that still possessed all the attributes that contributed to a successful career, successful parent, successful teammate, successful husband for 20 years, and successful person.

Emergence

My cocooning process was diminished because I did not have this framework or cycle established, and as you've read in this book, made for so many challenges with my transition. Even though I emerged from my cocoon not quite a fully formed new entity, I revisited the cocooning process multiple times that finally resulted in the emergence of a fully formed and functioning former Navy SEAL, exceptional parent, well rounded professional, emotionally intelligent and emotionally aware survivor and eventual best-selling author.

Resolution

Through it all, I had formed a new team, developed a new specialized expertise, gained a new tribe, asked for help, and finally received help. Looking back, I would not change my experience in any way.

There was a lot of pain, suffering, punishment, and disappointment. But what emerged was a better version of myself that couldn't have been realized without embarking on this journey and taking the leap of faith with a series of strategically placed guardians that handled my situation with a sense of care and delicacy because they somehow knew that I was in a fragile state and one wrong move could cause the entire work of art to crumble.

Once I emerged from the verge of breaking, those same guardians made demands of me that were sometimes harsh, at a pace that was much less comfortable than I would have preferred, and came at the price of hard work and perseverance.

Grief

Grief is the anguish experienced after a significant loss. The portion of the cycle that I was unaware of throughout the transition cycle of Isolation, Indulgence, Cocooning, Emergence, and Resolution was the very real need to identify that I was grieving.

I grieved the loss of my dad, my family, my friends and teammates, my life in the Teams, my identity, my expertise, the prestige of being a Navy SEAL, the lifestyle, the pace, the tragedies and triumphs.

All of these were dear and valued companions for decades, and the loss of some of them happened individually and over time. Most, however, happened instantly and at the same time on August 1, 2016, the day I retired from the Navy.

I wasn't prepared for the tumultuous nature of so many losses at once. There was no plan that could have ever prepared me for what I experienced at that moment when it was all over and I became a diminished sum of so many valued and cherished parts.

Whatever transition you're experiencing, you're going to go through it on your own terms and will develop your own cycle. Take the time to introspect your unique transition. Understand that you're going to have challenges and setbacks, but make the conscious effort to progress forward.

Anchor Points

Now that you have the framework for the transition cycle, I also want you to know that although my transition had some very real challenges, it was also full of some incredible and memorable moments. I was very deliberate to continue to do what makes me happy in what I call my "Anchor Points."

Aside from stepping off of the train and working at the best job in the best environment that I've ever worked in, I made a point to maintain discipline and remain open to opportunities by saying "yes" to just about everything.

Here is a small snapshot of the things that made every day memorable ...

The USC athletic staff and strength coaches allowed me complete access to the weightlifting facilities. Every day at 11:00, I would stop whatever I was doing at work and would go workout and absorb all the energy of so many young athletes working hard every day to perfect their craft and one day play their sport at the next level.

Although the students and I rarely interacted, they saw this old guy working hard every day and eventually word got out that a Navy SEAL was pushing weight at the gym, trying his hardest to fight off Father Time and keep his mind and body sharp.

Next, I would go to grab lunch and sit outside and enjoy the perfect Southern California weather, enjoy all the vibrancy of campus, all while basking in the warm embrace of this wonderfully nurturing environment.

Every weekend that I was in LA, I would go to the local coffee shop and order a coffee and sandwich and get down to the grueling necessity of studying as hard as I could to keep my head above water during my second attempt at graduate school.

Finishing the week tired and a bit weary, I still happily looked forward to catching the train on Monday and doing it all over again with all the good things that were my daily life as a student, former athlete, former Navy SEAL, and metamorphosing USC Trojan.

One part of my routine stands out more than all the rest. I was quickly becoming a creature of habit, and my routines were going against all the previous training of my previous life. I would get on the train at the same time. I would sit in the same car and try to get in the same spot for the hour-long commute to work.

Each morning from 2016 through 2020, I would listen to *The Dan Le Batard Show with Stugotz*. This sports show was a show about sports that rarely talked about sports. The show would eventually get around to the sports stories of the day, but for the most part, it was a show about a group of long-time friends that would make me laugh every morning.

Dan, Jon, Mike, Chris, Billy, and Roy had such great chemistry, and it felt like I was sitting in their living room experiencing the day with them. Needless to say, I would have at least one all-out laughing fit each morning. When I say laughing fit, I mean a laugh that starts in my stomach and radiates throughout my body, exploding out of my mouth at embarrassingly loud volumes for minutes at a time.

When I first started my new job, I worked there for about three months before I started my bi-weekly pilgrimage back to Virginia to visit and stay connected to my family. As I've mentioned earlier, LA is a big place and oftentimes not very friendly.

However, my routine had me surrounded by familiar faces that I affectionately called my "Train People." Although we didn't speak, we silently acknowledged each other with a friendly smile or nod and would go about our business on the long commute to work. Each morning, the silence was interrupted by my laughing fits that, unbeknownst to me, quickly spread throughout the car.

While I was in Virginia and away from my Train People, it turns out that I was sorely missed. I made it back to LA, and to my surprise, several of my people let out a gasp of relief and what I thought was happiness to see me. The lady that I sat next close to for those three months yelled, "He's back. The laughing man is back! We thought you left us."

I was taken completely by surprise because I thought I was just another commuter in a sea of commuters enduring the commute to work. I was sorely mistaken because my laughing fits made an entire section of the train join in on my happiness.

For almost four years, many of the faces changed, but many remained the same. Each morning, the entire car would quietly join me in my routine of uncontrolled laughter at my favorite show that helped me laugh when I wanted to sulk, beam when I wanted to be in a dark spot, and push on when I wanted to quit.

33

LESSONS LEARNED

"If you are distressed by anything external, the pain is not
due to the thing itself, but to your estimate of it; and this
you have the power to revoke at any moment."

—Marcus Aurelius

My life so far has been a story rich with transitions. Each chapter builds on the next one, and each chapter holds a lesson within it. There are some lessons that just keep. You learn them and you live them out again and again. I carry those lessons with me everywhere.

When you look for a way to learn from every transition, you grow. It's impossible to be stuck when you're growing.

Lean into your lessons and keep moving forward, eyes up. Eyes up because you need to see what's happening around you. You need to see others. And you need to use your lessons to lead them through the places you've already walked.

Take the First Step

Taking real action to be a Navy SEAL was my first transition with forward momentum. This may seem like a scary leap of faith or an act of courage, but that's not what it was for me.

Becoming a SEAL felt *safe* to me. Being a part of an elite U.S. military team didn't seem like a risk, it just seemed like a natural thing to do because I was third-generation military.

I truly believed that joining the SEALs was going to be my first step at redemption—redemption because it was going to be my clean slate. How crazy is that? I actually thought that earning a spot in one of the most elite military units in the world was a brand new chance to redeem myself.

But being a black man in the military means never having a clean slate. It means your slate has already been written on.

My military career began with not one but two strikes against me. I was obviously black. And I was also immediately considered inferior because of what is assumed that I "can't" do as a black man.

The fear of success is a real thing for me. In my mind, success comes with a ton of pressure. Even when I was playing football, I had a lot of anxiety playing a high-pressure position for my football team. No one would have guessed it, but being the center of attention was way outside my comfort zone. It was contrary to how I was raised.

My dad had taught me to be humble. As a young black kid, I learned never to call attention to myself. I know now that my dad used an approach of fear to parent me. He had good reason based on the culture around us. I know he just wanted us to stay safe and out of trouble.

That fear taught me something. My father and my life were teaching me that it was just better to blend in and not be seen. Nothing in me wanted to stand out.

I was playing college ball not because it was my passion but because my dad told me that I needed to get a college scholarship. Paying for college wasn't something my dad could manage. And I had no kind of plan, so I just went to college.

When that didn't work, I went from my familiar dysfunctional support system to *nothing*. I felt like I was transitioning *backward*. At the time, I had no framework to deal with how this backward transition was affecting me. No young man wants to transition down in life.

But what I eventually learned was that my first steps didn't need to carry the stigma of my past failings. And I just kept taking that next step forward.

Later, when Senior Chief Mink gave me that bottle of Bullfrog, that was the first time I was truly seen by someone at an elite level. Throughout my life, being seen hadn't been a good thing. Being seen meant too much attention or negative attention. It meant feeling horribly uncomfortable or facing some sort of punishment.

But Senior Chief Mink was a member of The Naval Special Warfare Development Group, at the top of his game, and he noticed me. He *saw* me. Someone significant in my life noticed me for a positive reason. He could see my value, my potential.

I had no clue that anybody was paying attention to me—especially not in a good way. Having this experience with Senior Chief Mink did something entirely new in me. It gave me a spark.

Do you know what happens when you're wiped out mentally and physically, but someone lights a seemingly insignificant spark? That little spark lights a flame inside of you. Sometimes you just need a spark to light a fire in your belly.

With that spark, I finally cleared the hurdle of uncertainty and moved forward to impress the instructor staff and dig deep down. Once you dig that deep, your perspective changes and your limits change.

I owe so much to that instructor staff … And as mean as the instructors could be, as hard as that course is, the instructors' job is to make sure that you get through the course.

They're going to give you every opportunity to pass. They're gonna give you every opportunity to fail. And it's up to each candidate to seek help, be humble, and get better every day.

Master Your Thoughts

One near-death experience is plenty, right? You don't go into the SEALs thinking you'll be avoiding dangerous situations. You *know* that your job is to go toward danger.

And still, I can't say that I expected to be launched overboard … It was a completely surreal experience—my second time facing death alone.

During my first near-death experience, it felt as if it was happening to me. I had no control. I was just hoping my training would work.

But this was the second time. This was entirely different. This time I wasn't hoping, I was pissed. I wasn't worrying about dying, I was plotting my revenge.

My body wasn't in fight or flight. I never even considered that death was going to happen. Internally, I knew I would be okay.

My mind wasn't racing. I was completely calm. I had the capacity to think my way through the problem, no matter my circumstances.

Work to be in control of your thoughts. When you master your mind, your feelings and your body will follow.

Climb the Rungs of Leadership

The transition to officer completely defined me as a leader. I was responsible for other people's lives, their families, and getting them back home during war.

OCS was practice because there were no real consequences for failures. But as the leader in a SEAL platoon we were no longer practicing, there were lives at stake. Every decision I made was about getting each of my guys home. And If I screwed up, somebody died.

These two years of my life were a culmination of all the lessons I had learned throughout my entire life and career in the Navy SEAL Teams. These two years didn't just begin two years ago. It started at the beginning of my story.

It started as a kid who felt different. It started as a kid who didn't fit.

Every lesson I learned was a different rung on the ladder, preparing me for this position of leadership.

No part of your life occurs in isolation from where you are now. Each experience contributes to the person you are and to the person you are becoming. Take everything that you have learned and turn it into rungs on your ladder to successful leadership.

Champion Others

True satisfaction comes as we help others navigate their own journeys. Witnessing their growth can be wonderfully fulfilling. Watching my students struggle, face their insecurities, and eventually grasp the knowledge and skills they sought, I had an innate sense of pride knowing that I got to have an impact on their lives.

As we champion others, it's important to exercise patience and understanding. What surprised me most along my journey is that I had thought that it would be my white counterparts who wouldn't want me to succeed. But in my case, the two people who didn't want me to succeed the most were not white.

It was a valuable lesson and one that I'll never forget. Unfortunately, throughout the course of my military career, there were plenty of people who weren't African American who wanted to make sure I didn't succeed in my career as an officer.

People you don't expect to advocate for you will surprise you and step up. And people you would expect to cheer you on will hold you down.

You will have opportunities for the rest of your life to be the person that helps someone succeed. Be the one who lifts others up, whose shoulders are broad enough to stand on.

Be Fully Present

Despite being away repeatedly on training trips that lasted for weeks or months at a time, I was a very involved dad. I wasn't neglectful. I can't even put into words how much I love being a dad.

Was it hard to be away from home? Yes. Was it hard coming back home and reconnecting with my baby girl? Yes. Was it hard to be gone while she was growing and changing without me there? Yes.

I thought because I was absent a lot that it made me a bad father. I was wrong. And I also learned that just because you don't know what you're doing as a dad, it doesn't mean you're doing it wrong.

I cherished every opportunity to reconnect with my daughter. I took it upon myself to establish a lot of firsts for the two of us. And I figured out what it means to be a connected dad. True connections are built to last.

Once Rylie recognized me as her dad, it changed everything. She became the most important thing in my life. It's an experience that I would never change. Becoming an active part of her life was a huge transition because before connecting, I felt like I wasn't needed and was only taking up space around her.

That first Daddy-Daughter date started a tradition for the two of us. Every Wednesday until she reached high school, she and I would go on a date. Those were the best two hours I spent with her.

It was just something that she and I could share. It was incredibly special, and I wouldn't trade that for anything.

I chose to do that with all four of my kids. But the first time you do something, it tends to be especially memorable.

Still, on Wednesdays, I want to be with her. Just this Wednesday, I actually had lunch with her. She's visiting from France. And it's the same thing I did with that small bit of effort as when she was a toddler.

It still goes on to this day. She's the same age now that I was when I decided to become a Navy SEAL. It was the best investment of time and focus that can never be replaced.

I went from being this smelly thing with a prickly face to somebody who she grew to know and love and respect. It's pretty spectacular the impact a moment can have. That one little moment when she smiled at me was the start of a beautiful relationship.

That transition, like all transitions, didn't turn out the way it looked at the beginning.

I tell that story to let parents know—especially fathers—that the special time you have with your child is short-lived, and before you know it, they're in their twenties, have graduated college, and are getting ready to be married.

I absolutely love being the father of four beautiful children. It's taught me so much, and I was able to pay it forward to all the rest of my children because I learned a lot from her. And I also taught her how she should be treated by her brother, her grandfather, her father, her boyfriend, and her husband.

That's the value of that time. And that consistency has brought me nothing but happiness throughout her life and the life of my other three children.

Your words, your actions, and your presence have an impact on someone's life. Being intentional with your impact creates a ripple effect that will carry out to even more people.

Accept Unexpected Invitations

Sniper school is a transition I did not want because it was something I didn't think I was qualified for. I wasn't a confident shooter, and it was such a hard school. It wasn't the hardest, but it was definitely the next to the hardest. And I just felt that I wasn't qualified for it.

If I could have done more time on the teams or just known it was coming and been able to prepare for it as opposed to ... "Hey, what are you doing?" It could have been anyone because they just needed a body.

That wasn't ideal for how I learn things. It caused a ton of anxiety as the inadequacy wound that's birthed from my childhood kicked up. If I had been able to prepare for it, it would have been easier.

The way it happened was not how I would have wanted to become a sniper. I didn't feel like I'd earned it. I just happened to be in the right place at the right time.

Sniper School is one of the elite programs available to SEAL Teams that is highly respected and sought after. Normally, people go through a selection process to have the opportunity to attend one of these programs. But in my case, I received an unexpected invitation.

During my first successful deployment, I had learned valuable lessons about leadership and special operations. Afterward, I had about six months to recover, reconnect with my family, participate in professional development, and then reintegrate back into my SEAL Team.

Professional development required us to go to specific schools to progress within the SEAL community. Of all the schools I knew were on the agenda, sniper school was the one I dreaded most. Being raised in Ohio, my gun interactions were limited. I didn't grow up hunting or heading to the shooting range for target practice.

Guns were foreign. And foreign didn't exactly scream, "Let's do this!" Snipers came with an intimidating reputation. Couple that reputation with their notoriously challenging missions, and that just left me feeling inadequate and woefully unqualified.

In my mind, I thought sniper school was something to put off. I thought that maybe in the future, when I had more experience under my belt in the SEAL community, sniper school could happen. But at that moment, as a newly minted SEAL, still learning and growing, it wasn't something I'd anticipated doing.

There are few jobs in the military or any other profession that require as much dedication, attention to detail, focus and perseverance as a special operator. There are the things that you see on TV or YouTube that give you a glimpse of the pain and suffering that are required to earn the right to perform at the highest levels and do the toughest job.

In a world of military specialization, there is a subset of people that do the silent and deadly job of a military sniper. When I try to explain that being deep in the desert, jungle, or any number of bad places in the world the one thing that is crucial in modern warfare is the United States sniper whose sole job is to take that "one" shot that can oftentimes change the balance of power on the modern battlefield. I was a Navy SEAL, but I was also a sniper.

The way it happened was completely unexpected, but it ended up being one of the most valuable experiences of my life. Sometimes you've got to trust someone else's faith in you and say yes to those invitations to step outside your comfort zone and into the unknown. There's an even better version of you waiting on the other side of that discomfort.

Figure It Out on the Go

Every speck of every extra moment spent learning my craft is deeply written into the grooves of my mind, my muscles, my spirit. But when I was put in charge of eighty-four scared and unprepared children during Officer Candidate School, I had no idea what I was doing.

I quickly realized that when people are in a leadership position, they don't always know exactly what to do. But those kids didn't know that I felt unprepared.

What I learned as their leader is that when the people around you don't bring their problems to you, that's a problem. People come to you with their problems when you are *not* failing them.

As a leader, you must look at the big picture. The people under you are focused on the smaller picture of the things right in front of them.

You don't have to know exactly what you're doing. You can still learn from people under you when you're open to it. I've learned more from the people I led than from those appointed over me who provided guidance, leadership, and examples of how to lead.

It was the young officers and enlisted who provided the best leadership guidance I've ever received.

To be a good leader, you must always leave your option open to also be a follower. Sometimes, your experience will bring out the things you already know about being a leader. Even when you don't feel confident, make a decision. Right or wrong, make a decision. The confidence will come.

As people watch you make your decisions, you are watching them. I watched each of my guys closely. Some of these SEALs were seen for the first time under my care.

Make the decision. Make the call. And make an effort to see the people in your care. There is power in seeing and being seen. As a leader, you must learn not only to see people but also to give them—and yourself—a clean slate.

Reconnect and Restore Relationships

When my dad started treatment, I was assigned to a sniper cell in Indiana that was only two hours from my old house in Dayton, Ohio. This enabled me to repair and reconnect the relationship with my dad.

Rather than not knowing who I was, or being the invisible middle child, I became my dad's rock.

Growing up, my dad saw me as disrespectful, defiant, and always questioning everything. He didn't understand how I learned. He didn't understand that all of my questions were my way of understanding whatever situation I was in. To my dad, my questions just made me seem like a mouthy kid.

I guess you could say my dad wasn't an even-tempered disciplinarian. He often directed that temper at the child who drove him crazy with questions.

I learned that I had to be invisible because I was a defiant child and because my dad would bully me if I brought too much attention to myself. I became comfortable acting stoic, shrinking myself down, and blending into the background.

So, when my dad was in treatment, I had a decision to make. Would I choose to keep the distance between us? Or would I open my heart to my dying father?

I opened my heart and allowed space for restoration.

What I can tell you is that when you have an opportunity to restore or repair an important relationship, you have to make space for it mentally, emotionally, and physically. And know that relational restoration will help you grow as a person and free up space in your heart and mind for healing and growth.

I was so heartbroken that I had to be the one who made the decision to take my dad's leg. Yet I knew that this surgery was the only way to save his life. I also believed he was going to be angry with me. But my dad wasn't mad.

It felt so good to be pleasantly surprised by my dad's reaction. I also came face to face with the reality that my father didn't know the man I had become.

Seek the Truth

Two years prior to finishing my career in the military, reality started to set in. That's when I had to take an evaluation of all the things necessary to close out my career—and when I found out the "why" behind what was happening in my mind and body. It registered with me that I wouldn't have enough tools to make it without taking advantage of the help available to me.

When I got my test results, it was a relief. I could tell something wasn't quite right. The test results validated those unspoken suspicions.

When you suspect something is wrong with you, your first step is to figure out what that thing is. You have to be curious enough to muster the courage to find out so you can live your life.

Life outside of the military seemed terrifying because I didn't know my worth to anybody on the outside. Nothing that I had done seemed to translate to civilian life. In the Locker Room, I was constantly surrounded by excellence, dominating every challenge I faced, doing everything at full speed. Every aspect of life in the Teams is a No Fail Mission, and those dynamics are unique and specific to the SEAL Teams and Special operations throughout the military.

My best bit of advice to anybody getting out of the SEALs is that you can never recreate the SEAL life or the SEAL "Locker Room." Even to this day, nothing I've ever experienced has come close to that Locker Room.

But you can recreate community.

Keep Moving

When I was almost two years into my transition out of the SEALs, I had gone through what felt like repeated transitions. I was making progress on the work side of things, but I absolutely could not keep my marriage together.

I was moving forward in so many ways, but I often felt like I was spinning my wheels. No matter how many positive steps I took toward my career change, the state of my marriage seemed to be going in reverse. I just couldn't win in marriage.

Even though I still hadn't mastered how to transition successfully, I was incrementally moving forward in the middle of my setbacks.

Incrementally. Increments are relative. They are not a specific, consistently measurable thing. Every speck you move in a positive direction is an increment. Every mile you move is an increment. Over time, you'll see your progress. Just keep moving.

Expose Unhealed Wounds

I'd been in a dysfunctional family support system, but it was still my team. Then, I was on a college football team. And after that, I was on a SEAL Team. In one way or another, my entire life I had been a part of a team.

And then I wasn't. It was time for me to go it alone. I was transitioning from a team to being solo. I was transitioning from a consistent presence of support to what felt like a support vacuum.

Sometimes, when you've been living life at a level eight on the high-alert, high-pressure scale, and then you're moved to a safe space, your body finally feels the freedom to let all of the anxiety come out.

I didn't want to let it out, but that energy had to go somewhere. Ultimately, I had no choice. I had to deal with my invisible injuries, or they would have their way with me. I couldn't let that happen if I was going to move forward.

Whatever your invisible injuries may be, you can bank on them making an appearance in some form. Isolation primes you for being vulnerable to unhealed wounds. Unhealed wounds fester. You must do the work to find your unhealed wounds so you can heal.

Embrace Grief

The hours that passed while I silently held the knowledge that Michael was gone until his wife could be told ... Those were the hardest twenty-four hours I have ever experienced.

Nothing in my training could have prepared me for that tragedy. It was the first time in my life I had lost someone outside of my immediate family who was family to me. And I would never be the same.

All these years later, I am still recovering. There are some transitions that take such a painful toll that they require years and years to process.

The awful lingering pain of grief mingles with unanswered questions and what-ifs ... *What else could I have done? I should have ... What if I ...?*

It's taken me a long time to get here, but I've finally learned to let myself grieve. I don't have a magic message to help anyone transition through grief. You just have to feel it, you have to walk in it.

Give yourself the gift of embracing grief. It's the path to healing.

Talk to Strangers

When I decided to go to New York City for that fundraising event and I met Mr. McMorrow, at the time, our conversation seemed random and out of the blue. But that meeting changed my life in ways that I still feel.

I believe that I'm able to write this book because that one person cared so much about my well-being and my next steps that he would not accept my failing to live up to my full potential. He had the influence, access, and reach to help with my transition, and I'm forever grateful.

There are not enough words to express how grateful I am for the time he took with me and my family to make that transition as smooth as possible. But with so many moving parts, there were going to be some challenges and unforeseen things that happened that seemed insurmountable. That was unavoidable.

Looking back on it, like so many challenges in life, making the journey through it was the hard part. Once I emerged on the other side, I was better for it. I was more experienced.

Of course, I may have gained a couple more scars as a result, but I also had a new path, a new purpose, a new team, and new goals to strive for.

Years later, I can clearly see that meeting, that one person, that stranger who cared enough to make sure that my transition was simply a segue into a new phase of my life, not only my life but also the life of my family.

You never know who's watching or paying attention to you. Your effort matters. Your effort reflects character and reveals potential—even when you can't see it. People around you can see things in you that you're blind to and call them out.

Avoid Prolonged Isolation

USC gave me what I didn't even know I needed—belonging. I *knew* I belonged at this amazing place. I had found my tribe, my team, my locker room.

It was as if the campus wrapped its arms around me. The people embraced me and claimed me as one of their own. That kind of support gave me legs to stand on.

Finding your tribe is so important—especially when you're feeling isolated and dealing with unhealed wounds or invisible injuries. Even if you can't find a tribe, find a way to *not* go through major changes along. Long-term isolation is not your friend.

Accept Help

I was terrified that people would learn I flunked out of college and I'd be labeled as dumb. I had to take that fear and process it by asking myself all the questions running roughshod all over my mind.

This was when I understood that people who've reached a certain level in their careers just want you to succeed. They aren't threatened by your potential. And they don't let your past determine your future. This type of person wants to know who you really are and what you're made of.

I had to get over my fear of inadequacy.

I had to be willing to take the hand that was offered to me.

I had to learn that there are people who genuinely want to help.

In order to achieve something, you have to be willing to be uncomfortable. You have to accept that you won't achieve things in isolation—to ask for help and take it when it's offered.

Help can come from anywhere. Be open to help from wherever it comes. Vulnerability is a good thing. It's a gift that leads to healing and growth.

Take the Growth Path

I had originally thought of joining the FBI because it was an easy button. I'd still be able to do cool stuff. It would be a team-oriented job, so I could be somewhat SEAL-ish.

I realize that the FBI sounds like an exciting job. But I had been an elite Navy SEAL. The FBI would be just another day at the office for me. And I was willing to settle.

It was easier to settle than to do the work to find out what I could be good at outside of my SEAL career. It would force me to face doubts I didn't really want to look at.

It's a hard reality to face the idea that you might not be good at anything else other than being a SEAL. I had no idea how being a sniper could translate into real life.

The easiest path is not always the best path. Be willing to take the path that requires you to grow.

"Are you willing to sprint when the distance is unknown?"

—Lewis Caralla

Questions to Help You Get UNSEALED

When is the last time you were intentionally quiet?

If you sit still long enough with no distractions, no mental diversions, just quiet … What takes over? What intrusive thoughts take hold of your mind? You know those thoughts, those memories. They're the ones that won't leave you alone. They're the ones you've been shoving down.

They're the thoughts that don't come alone. They come with pain. Is it in your chest? Your clenched jaw? The back of your neck? Your gut? Or maybe your hips are tight?

Pain that's kept in the dark is pain that grows in the dark.

Your first transition begins in your mind. You have to make a decision to face yourself and the pain that comes with the looking. Face the part of you that keeps you stuck, the thing that won't let you grow.

I can't tell you what that is. I can just show you ways to transition well and keep moving forward.

Every morning, write down the things you're thankful for. Taking your gratitude into daily account will be the catalyst for shifting your mindset. Get a notebook, get a journal, do whatever it takes to make this into a daily habit.

Recall a really hard time at the beginning of your journey. Think about where you were then and take a look at where you are now. Write it all down. Revisit those moments a month from now, a year from now. Track your progress. *You are remarkable.*

Your mind and body are so much stronger and more capable than you've ever thought.

Transition is a process. It not only affects the individual but also the entire family. It's a journey that is unique to each person, but there are similarities that so many of us face.

If I've learned anything from navigating my own transitions, it's that the worst way to embark on this journey is to try to do it alone. I've had so much help from baristas to billionaires, and each level of support was part of my lifeline that has allowed me to share these experiences with you.

The muscles that I used to solve problems on my own have long since atrophied because I've relied on my teammates or other members of my support team so much that I'm no longer good at doing things on my own.

Look around at the people in your life that love and support you and ask them for help. The first step is so often the hardest, but it's by far the most important decision and gift you can give yourself and your loved ones.

Even though transitions of all types come with their own unique challenges, the thread that all significant transitions have in common is their difficulty. There are certainly levels of difficulty, but they are all difficult in their own way.

My journey shows how and why I struggled with so many of my transition obstacles, but more importantly, highlights my ability to recognize that I needed help and my willingness to ask for the help I needed.

The people that stepped in to help me are some of the most amazing people I've ever met. My life would be completely different if these guardian angels weren't with me at the right place and the right time.

If you feel isolated, please reach out for help. Support is out there. No matter which direction you're transitioning, you don't need to transition alone.

> "You gain strength, courage and confidence by every experience in which you really stop to look fear in the face. You are able to say to yourself, 'I have lived through this horror. I can take the next thing that comes along.' You must do the thing you think you cannot do."
>
> **—Eleanor Roosevelt**

ACKNOWLEDGMENTS

I can't believe that I've finished my first book. This has been an unexpected labor of love that began over 25 years ago. As with many things that end a lot larger and more grandiose than their humble beginnings, I first told my story at the Smithsonian Institute way back in 2009.

Naval Special Warfare had an initiative that demanded that their officers learn to speak comfortably in public as representatives of the Navy and speak coherently to top leadership at home and on deployment. I was one of six speakers and as each speaker ended their speech, I still didn't have a clue as to what to talk about.

I didn't feel my story was very interesting. Each minute that passed left me reeling about what to say. I looked around and realized the audience was mostly comprised of young men who had aspirations of becoming Navy SEALs. As I was being introduced, it finally hit me. I asked myself what I would want to hear if I were in their shoes. I decided I'd like to hear some cool stories about BUD/S, life as a SEAL, and a cool war story.

Fortunately, I had just the thing for the young audience. As I did my best to entertain and inspire, I felt clumsy and slightly awkward, but they had no idea it was my first time addressing a crowd.

Admittedly, I had a little help from a very nice woman who was sitting next to me. Her husband spoke just before me. During his speech, she leaned over very excitedly and asked what I was going to speak about. I answered honestly that I wasn't quite sure yet.

In the most encouraging and hushed tone she said, "Just don't be boring like the guy speaking now." She gave me a small wink and put her finger to her lips in a gesture of keeping a secret. I hope he doesn't read this and find out the true secret of my first successful speech.

Fast forward to 2023, and my humble beginnings with an inventory of very few stories, and very little confidence as a public speaker has blossomed into a book that I am very proud of and hope you've enjoyed reading.

I would love to take most of the credit for this book, but as with so much of my life story, I had a significant amount of help. Pivotal Moments Media and their CEO Bob Morgan had so much faith in me that he basically forced me to tell my story in the form of a book because he truly believed that my story could help a lot of people experiencing their own metamorphosis.

One day, Bob had enough of my stalling and told me that the book was a go and to get started right away and it's a mission that I have to complete. That's when a hidden gem of a "Co-writer" entered my life by the name of Shelby Rawson.

Shelby has done such an amazing job of taking my story and breathing life into it and adding what I affectionately call "Texture" to my narrative. Truth be told, I tell stories much better than I write them, and Shelby did an incredible job of refining my block of clay by molding it, shaping it, and creating order out of chaos. I couldn't dream of a better partner than Shelby to help shape and craft our book.

Next, the "Architect" Lori Lynn added so many layers by changing my sledgehammer into a scalpel that guides the reader through my journey with precision as the audience meanders effortlessly through each story every step of the way. Lori and Shelby had no problem pushing me to add more emotion here, dive much deeper there, and keep the vision of the book in full focus while I did my "Homework" to make our final product something that we could all be proud of.

Up to this point, most of my writing was academic and didn't require the level of emotional depth that this book demanded. Lori knew that I needed the reader to accompany me and that experience must have depth, character, and vulnerability. Almost like plugging into Mark Greene's very own version of *The Matrix*, all of Lori and Shelby's expertise and guidance added so much breadth to each facet and layer of this book and then Justin Palm closed us out with a solid proofread.

Finally, thank you to Shanda Trofe, along with her dedicated team at Transcendent Publishing, who worked tirelessly getting *UNSEALED* beautifully designed and ready to publish.

Thank you all for the behind-the-scenes work and perseverance that was greatly appreciated from day one. I believe that this book belongs to all of us, and I know you're all as proud of *UNSEALED* as I am.

There are so many people that I need to thank for making the dream of writing a book become a reality, and now that it's really here, thanking all of the people in my life seems only fitting since you've made my life an incredibly enriched and fulfilled experience.

I'd like to thank my family and friends who have supported me throughout my life. Thank you Rylie Greene, Braden Greene, Evan Greene, Olivia Greene, Esther Lee Greene, Anthony Greene, and Stacy Greene. My Aunt Catherine Woodard, Uncle Willie Woodard, Nathan P. Woodard, Marcus Woodard, and David Woodard. My Aunt Diane Walker, Leslie Walker, Mark Walker, Eric Walker, and Christopher Walker. William, Tammy, Celeste, and Spencer Voss. Vaughan and Joy Walls. My best friend since I was eighteen, Ryan DeVoe, and his amazing wife and children Sara, Tatum, Crew, Tinley, Micah, and Team DeVoe.

Thank you to my mentors and Guardian Angels William McMorrow and Kent Mouton, without you, life after retirement wouldn't have been so rewarding. My SEAL partner in crime Greg Sisa and his lovely wife Paige. Jeff and Suzanne Turner, the staff and employees of Kennedy Wilson.

Thank you to Albert Checcio, Bob Morgan, Doug Byers, Tracey Vranich, Sara Trudell-McCoy, Mark Kenneth Todd, Kathleen Erikson, John Carlsson (JC), Ashley Merryman, Rhea Mac, Peggy Mathews, Tyler Espinoza, Todd Owen, Regina Nordahl, Glenn Fox; Joseph, Batsheva, Michael, Yakov, Esti, Rachel, Yehuda, and Moshe Judah; Brenden Leary, Rich Diviney, Patrick McGee, Michael Holt, Rob Matarese, Eric Donahue, David Gooch, Greg Simons, Matt Espindola, Mark Owen, George Petersen, Steve Hohl, Jared Albair, Andrew Stumpf, Drew Ellis, Jay Manty, Jeff Stihl, Malcolm Murray, Jeff Williams, Bruce Schlieman, Shannon

Murphy, Ryan Dick, Angel Naves, JD Donaldson, Rob Kaneiss, Adam Pietrzak, Derek Petrin, Cameron Hamilton, Jerry Shick, Ted LeCouffe, Brent Jorgensen, Mike Baas, Chad Voodren, Todd Owen, Matt McGraw, Daniel Barkhuff, Harrold Fannell, Devon Grube (RIP), Harley Beville, Misti Pace, Belisa Del Conte, Coach Clay Helton, Julie Elder, Arwen Duffy, Jake DeVine, Dave Carrera, Josh Heidegger, Calen Ouellette, Pivotal Moments Media, Shelby Rawson, Lori Lynn, Shanda Trofe, Transcendent Publishing, Dr. Patrick Joyner, Kevin Ellerbe, Terry Carter, Jim Clement, Mike Sterling, Jeff Chabot, Andrew and Jennifer Grooms, Bobby Kilpatrick, Tommy Wang, Nicole Pizzingrilli, Morey Norris, Brian Miller, Kevin Pong, Chris Zachritz, Steve Zynda, Steven Barrett, Kelley Harcourt, Booker Figgins, David, Jerry and Dennis Wamsley, Kenya Burrell, Kevin Williams, Jerome, Kevin, and Keith Hopson, Derrick Austin, Glenn Jonnson, Irene Lang-Kleiman, Dennis Perkins, Berkeley Claggett, Sean Huffman, Chuck Edwards, Juan Brown, Jeffrey Cooks, Byron Hurst, Star Hurst, Nicole Brown, Robert Andrews, Matt Stevens.

Thank you Dan Le Batard, Jon "Stugotz" Weiner, Mike Ryan Ruiz, Chris Cote, Roy Bellamy, Billy Gill, and Gonzalo Le Batard (Papi) from *The Dan Le Batard Show with Stugotz* for being the bright spot for so much of my transition. I can't thank you enough for all the laughs and antics.

The world's biggest shout-out to the University of Southern California (the world's greatest University and greatest 400,000+ Alums) and the brave men and women of the Army, Navy, Air Force, Marines, and Coast Guard that served honorably and defended this great nation. The Green Berets, Marine Raiders, Special Warfare Combat Crewmen (SWCC), Air Force Combat

Control Teams (CCT), the Navy SEAL Teams, and all US Tier ONE Units keeping America safe.

Thank you to Dr. Tom Holovacs, JD Wilson, Russ Romano, Tom Dietz, David Thomas, Ollie and Florida Thomas, Amy Crowder, Deena Kemper, Jeri DeAnn Beal, Jeremy Wilson, Rachel Wilson, Nella Sue Wilson, Mrs. Naomi O'Reilly, Mr. Kevin O'Hearn, Coach Jim Place, Coach Gradlin Pruitt, Coach Jack Johnson, Coach Jeff Fanscher, Coach Pete Cordelli, Coach Randy Walker (RIP), Joe Napoli, Jeremy Patterson, Brian Besse, Chris Ondrula, Rob (Bobby Gas) Echols, William Browning.

USC Trojans ... Fight On!!

PHOTO GALLERY

Coronado, California
Sunday July 28th, '02

I have just spent the best part of two days interviewing and quizzing MARK L. Greene, Age 30, ABH2/E/5 SC-- --- For selection to an Active Duty Reserve Commission. As a man in his early '20's, he attended Varsity Football Training Camps at Miami University, Oxford, Ohio and at an early Age, and Kent State the following year. A towering Youth, at over 6 feet 3", a durable prospect, he ran into injury problems at Both colleges. He became discouraged, Joined The Navy, and prevailed over his confident stature throughout a decade of petty-officer service. This Thick Account describes a man committed to The SEAL ethic and Total dependability at every juncture.

Commander Dean Laird, a comparison aviator with me for years, urged me to get acquainted with a totally committed SEAL with over a decade of experience. Mark Greene's motivation and dependability struck me exactly as it did Dean Laird. [Dean Laird is currently President of The American Fighter Aces Association.] This man will will Rise as a Model for his contemporaries. He currently holds a Bachelor of Arts degree from Excelsior College's Branch at San Diego SEAL Headquarters. He is Married, a Model husband, with 2 Young children. I seek advice on the Route to take, for that Appointment. Jim Stockdale

The handwritten letter of recommendation from Admiral Stockdale

Top Row: Aaron Adair, Anthony Greene
Bottom Row: Mark Greene, Nathan Woodard

Mark Greene and Matt Horn: Terrified on First Day of First Phase

Jack Carr, Ryan Dick, Michael Bearden, and Mark Greene

Mark's Marauders at 10,000 feet

Helicopter Sniper Training (Denmark)

Leaving the Wire with EOD in Afghanistan

With My USC Family: Greg and Paige Sisa; Kent Mouton; Mark Greene; Bill McMorrow; Bob, Rachel, and Robert Clifford

Mark Greene and Kent Mouton: Fight On!!!

Mark Greene and Bill McMorrow

Recording in the Studio with Pivotal Moments Media

"One of the greatest discoveries a man makes, one of his great surprises, is to find he can do what he was afraid he couldn't do."

—Henry Ford

ABOUT THE AUTHOR

Mark Greene is a retired Navy SEAL officer and sniper, former college athlete, speaker, and father of four who has mastered the slippery slope of transition while facing extreme pressure, loss, and countless life changes.

After an injury closed the door on his football career, Mark's path led him on a journey to a Navy SEAL career. To make life more exciting, the same year he graduated from SEAL training, he also became a first-time father.

In the years to follow, he was deployed to Pacific Theater SEAL Team FIVE and returned home to find himself battling his way through Sniper School, only to graduate as the first-ever African American Navy SEAL Sniper. He followed that up by being a sniper instructor and fathering his second child.

Over the next fourteen years, Mark would become the dad to two more children and continue to advance his military career as an officer.

He served as:

- Assistant Officer in Charge, SEAL Team EIGHT, deployed to Iraq Operation Iraqi Freedom
- Officer in Charge, Special Boat Team TWENTY
- Officer in Charge, SEAL Team EIGHT, deployed to Afghanistan Operation Enduring Freedom
- Special Boat Team TWENTY Operations Officer
- Special Operations Command Europe (SOCEUR), deployed to Afghanistan Operation Enduring Freedom
- Naval Special Warfare Group FOUR

In the middle of missions, chaos, and fatherhood, Mark graduated from the Naval Postgraduate School with his MBA in Financial Management and earned the Outstanding Thesis Award.

Twenty years of service later, he joined the President's Staff for Veteran Support at the University of Southern California and earned another degree, his USC Master's of Public Policy. And although Mark no longer works at USC, he returns regularly to deliver inspiring speeches to their highest-achieving students.

Mark Greene has learned that transitioning is a lifelong process and learning to do it well helps you to face your past, live in your present, and walk well into your future.

YOU ARE NOT ALONE

"A lot of people resist transition and therefore never allow themselves to enjoy who they are. Embrace the change, no matter what it is; once you do, you can learn about the new world you're in and take advantage of it."

—Nikki Giovanni

Every day, 22 veterans take their own lives. When I made this discovery, a spark ignited within me, and I knew we needed to get it published and into the hands of as many people as possible—as quickly as possible. Something had to be done, and there was no time to lose.

This book is a labor of love, and it's intended to help those who are struggling with major life changes.

There's something terrifying about transitioning—be it transitioning to a new job or transitioning from a sports career, or transitioning from single to married. All transitions come at a cost and if you're not prepared for the transition like I was unprepared, it can be a daunting and scary experience.

While this book may be about how a high-achieving Navy SEAL struggled with transition, it's written with you in mind. If you're personally experiencing the difficulties that come with growth and change, give yourself some well-deserved grace and realize that you are valuable, not a burden, and have everything it takes to successfully navigate the next chapter in your life.

For more resources on ways to adjust and adapt through the different seasons of change, visit:

Pivotal Moments Media | PIvotalMomentsMedia.com

EMDR International Association Home/EMDR Practitioners | endria.org

The Headstrong Project | theheadstrongproject.org

The Institute of Sports Performance | tinssp.com

If you know someone who is facing the challenges of transition, please consider sharing a copy of this book with them. You can help more people find out about *UNSEALED* simply by leaving a rating and review. Your words have the power to help reach those who are struggling and need a lifeline.

CONNECT WITH MARK

If you'd like to discuss any of the ideas in this book, please reach out to me by email. You can write to me at markgreeneauthor@gmail.com. I would love to know what parts of the book had the most impact on you. I also welcome your suggestions for getting our loved ones through some of the biggest changes in their lives—together.

themarkgreene.com